SUSPICIOUS MINDS

BEN RANDALL

SUSPICIOUS MINDS
First published August 2020
Revised February 2021

Content warning:
This story contains references to sexual abuse and violence.

Some names have been changed to conceal identities.
The author does not advocate any methods used herein
to contact or meet with victims of human trafficking.
Vietnamese characters are presented without diacritics.
Prices quoted in the text are given in US dollars,
unless stated otherwise.

No part of this work is to be reproduced or shared, in any form
or by any means, without the author's prior written consent.

ISBN (PDF): 978-0-6487573-3-7
ISBN (Paperback): 978-0-6487573-4-4
ISBN (epub): 978-0-6487573-5-1

Learn more at
www.sistersforsale.com

This book is dedicated to the truth,
whatever it may cost

CONTENTS

"If a man meets a virgin who is not betrothed, and seizes her and lies with her, and they are found, then the man who lay with her shall give to the father of the young woman fifty shekels of silver, and she shall be his wife."

- Deuteronomy 22:28-29

INTRODUCTION

'Suspicious Minds' is the second part of the incredible true story behind the multi-award-winning documentary, 'Sisters for Sale'.

Young women on the border between Vietnam and China find themselves caught between a violent custom and a vicious criminal underworld.

Investigating the mysterious disappearances of his local friends May and Pang, an Australian filmmaker uncovers a human trafficking crisis and sparks an amazing series of events.

Betrayed, kidnapped, and forced into marriage with strangers, May and Pang – still only teenagers – are forced to make the heartbreaking choice between their baby girls and their own freedom.

Since its premiere in Italy in November 2018, 'Sisters for Sale' has won awards and acclaim at film festivals around the world for exceptional filmmaking and courageous storytelling. It has now been translated into more than a dozen languages – an extraordinary feat for such a small production.

'Sisters for Sale' is a five-year story. Each of the books can be read independently: reading part one is not essential to understanding part two.

In the first book, 'Every Stranger's Eyes', Ben meets May and Pang, learns of their subsequent abductions, and returns to Vietnam determined to do everything he can to find and help them.

Part two, 'Suspicious Minds', covers Ben's investigation in Vietnam, from January to April 2014.

The third part of the story, 'The Man's Machine', follows the climactic search for May and Pang in China.

The author, Ben Randall, is an Australian activist and acclaimed documentary filmmaker.

His work has been seen and heard by millions of people around the world via new and traditional media - including CNN, Discovery Asia, Newsweek, TEDx, VICE, ABC, CBC, Channel NewsAsia, VTV, Walk Free, Freedom United, Imgur, and Reddit.

The books and documentary are all part of 'The Human, Earth Project', a non-profit grassroots organisation founded by the author in 2013.

All sales help fund the fight against the global human trafficking crisis. Additional contributions make a real difference and are always welcome at humanearth.net.

SUSPICIOUS MINDS

PART TWO OF THE INCREDIBLE TRUE STORY BEHIND THE ACCLAIMED 'SISTERS FOR SALE' DOCUMENTARY

GHOST TOWN

Three and a half years after my departure from Sapa, I returned to that realm of mist and fog nestled amongst Vietnam's northern mountains.

The first time I'd come to Sapa was in May 2010. I'd arrived there on holidays, as a backpacker. Sapa was supposed to be a brief stop on a three-year journey through Asia – until, almost by accident, it had become my home.

It was in Sapa that I'd first met the Black Hmong people, an impoverished tribal group struggling to survive in the rugged borderlands between Vietnam and China.

The Vietnamese Hmong people lived in a world of ghosts and monsters. They believed in shapeshifters, invisible things, and hairy little devils that herded tigers in the forest. They warned each other against tall, silent creatures that would rise from rivers to seize noisy children, beasts that sucked the blood of pigs, and the deranged woman with dog's teeth who devoured unattended babies.

It was incredible how little attention the Hmong people seemed to give to the true monster in their midst. Each year, many dozens of their sisters and daughters were being snatched and stolen away, to be sold to strangers in distant lands.

Sapa was in the throes of a major human trafficking crisis – and the strongest response from the local community seemed to be shaming and blaming the victims.

While I'd lived in Sapa, there had been a group of ten teenage Hmong girls who often sat on the corner of my street, selling handicrafts to tourists. We laughed and joked together every day – and, in time, I became friends with several of them.

Within twenty months of my departure from Sapa, no less than five of those ten girls were kidnapped in separate incidents.

There was one girl in particular who had always been the centre of attention, and had become my closest friend in the group: a tiny fourteen-year-old named May, who had a big smile, a big mouth, and a big heart.

It was now January 2014 – two and a half years since May's mysterious disappearance. I was returning to Sapa to find out what had happened to her: but I quickly realised that Sapa was a very strange place to search for the truth.

Sapa was a viper's nest of rumours. I was amazed how difficult it was to establish even the most basic facts in this world of superstition, gossip, and small-town intrigue.

Almost everyone in Sapa seemed to have a secret, or a hidden motive; it might be something innocent, or it could be something far more sinister. The locals were scared – of the traffickers, of the authorities, and of each other. Every time I heard a story it changed, often dramatically, and truth was entangled with fantasy. I had to sift through myriad distortions, lies, and rumours to get at the bare facts beneath.

The Hmong people had a very fluid sense of time and place, and often lost track of days, months, and years. There were no maps or calendars here, and few people could read or write. Apart from an occasional yellowing document, or a handful of old photographs tacked to a wall or tucked away in a purse, the only way to access the past was through memory. It was impossible to find out exactly when my friends had been kidnapped, or even when they'd been born.

As one friend put it, "Hmong people don't count. We don't have birthdays. People don't know how old they are, they're just guessing."

Someone might tell me, with absolute certainty, that May had been kidnapped in July – only to change their mind a moment later and assure me it was, in fact, August. When I asked which day of the week she'd been taken, I got answers like, "maybe Tuesday or Saturday".

Officially, the Vietnamese used the Gregorian calendar, as did most of the world – but they were also influenced by the Chinese calendar, which was based on the cycles of the sun and the moon.

In the villages outside Sapa, however, the sense of time was tied to the seasons: the planting season, the warm rainy season, the harvest, and the brutally cold winter. These were the hazy landmarks the local people used to orient themselves in time.

It could be incredibly difficult to tell who was related to whom, and how. The locals referred to distant relatives as cousins, to cousins as sisters and brothers, and to family friends as aunts and uncles. There was a rumour that May's family was not her real family, that they'd actually bought her as a child.

There were intense jealousies and rivalries even between close friends. I struggled to read people's true emotions, and to understand why they laughed at tragedies that tore families apart. Terrible truths lay concealed in vague expressions.

If a girl disappeared, it was often assumed with shocking rapidity that she had "gone to China", where she was beyond the reach of anyone who might want to help her.

The facts my Hmong friends related were further distorted by their erratic use of the English language. They struggled to describe certain things, and would often invent or substitute words. More complex ideas could easily become lost or confused. My friends would muddle their past, present, and future tenses, wreathing their stories in a fog of uncertainty.

I was accompanied in Sapa by a European cameraperson, Marinho, who was recording my investigations for a documentary we were producing. I interviewed dozens of people, both on and off camera, to learn all I could about the local human trafficking crisis, and quickly realised that the puzzle was far more complex than I could have imagined. Some of the pieces took months to fall into place, while others will never be found.

Many of the Hmong people shared the same names, and others were confusingly similar. Many were known by different names to different people. Just among the people involved in my investigation, there were Chu, Chu, Khu, Khu, Zu, Giu, Vu, Vu, Shu, Sho, Cho, Cho, Chan, Chinh, Chinh, Dinh, Dinh, Phinh, Pang, Pang, Cang, Lung, Dung, Ha, Ta, Xa, Xa, Xay, Nay, May, May, May, My, Zy, Zao, Zao, and Bao.

As I plunged ever-deeper into the swirling, ever-shifting labyrinth of lies and rumours, I realised there was just one piece of concrete information in Sapa that could give me any real hope of ever finding May.

That information was being jealously guarded by May's own father – and, as my investigation pushed forward, he was to do everything in his power to stop me from getting it.

Before my work was over, May's family was

threatening to have me killed for trying to help their daughter.

I wasn't on holidays anymore.

DAZED AND CONFUSED

If this was a fictional story, it would have a small number of distinctive characters, and a neatly-structured plot.

In reality, however, my investigation in Sapa was an incredibly complex one, involving many Hmong people with very similar names, and many interwoven threads. In telling the story here, I've untangled and separated out some of those threads, to make them easier to follow.

My Hmong friends were part of a group of ten girls, which included:

— May (a bright, fearless girl and my closest friend within the group, now a victim of human trafficking),

— Zao (a highly perceptive girl, May's cousin and closest friend),

— Pang (a moody, moon-faced girl, now a victim of

human trafficking),

— Vu (something of an outsider within the group, now a survivor of human trafficking),

— Chu (a sweet, serious girl, the only one of the group to pursue a university education),

— Little Chu (a cheerful girl, now married in Sapa, whose family had converted to Christianity),

— Chan (a very intelligent girl whom we are yet to meet),

— Ha (May's cousin, who had alerted me to May's first contact from China),

— Cho (May's elder sister, whom I'd known only slightly, also a victim of human trafficking), and

— Shu (a survivor of human trafficking, whom I'd never known well).

We'll also meet:

— Chinh (May's boyfriend at the time of her abduction),

— Xa (another friend of May, Zao, and Pang's),

— Big Zao (Vu's aunt, also a survivor of human trafficking),

— Dinh (May's eldest sister, now married with children),

— Dung and Lung (May's mother and father, respectively), and

— Bao (Pang's mother, a widow).

I also had Vietnamese friends in Sapa of the dominant Kinh ethnic group, who were not involved in my investigation. The most prominent among these were:

— Toan (a very close friend and chef at the Yellow Dragon hotel and restaurant, where I'd lived and taught English in 2010), and

— Huong (one of my former students, now married to Toan and living at the Yellow Dragon).

It's not nearly as confusing as it seems, I promise – and if you get lost, you can always come back here.

SUSPICIOUS MINDS

One week before my return to Sapa, I'd received some incredible news.

For the first time since her abduction, May had made contact from China, where she'd been forced into marriage and motherhood. For the first time, there was real hope of bringing May home to her family in Vietnam.

In Hanoi, I'd met with an Australian man named Michael Brosowski. Michael was the founder of Blue Dragon Children's Foundation, an organisation that had rescued dozens of trafficked Vietnamese girls from China.

I'd given May's Chinese number to Michael, so he could begin the process of carefully reaching out to her, trying to better understand her situation, and – hopefully – organising her rescue.

Michael had continually emphasised the need for slow, deliberate action.

"If you mess up one of these cases, it could result in a girl being killed," he'd told me. "It's that serious."

But I had messed up, almost immediately. We'd lost all contact with May and, with it, perhaps the only chance we'd ever have to help her.

There was no way of knowing what danger May might now be in. We might never hear from her again, and might never know what had happened to her.

May's cousin and best friend Zao had told me that May had been sold in China by a young Hmong man. My last remaining hope of finding May was to identify that man, and to find out what he knew. If I could learn where he'd sold May, and to whom, I'd be one step closer to finding her.

There was an extremely slender chance of success, if there was any chance at all. I'd be hunting the hunters, playing a cat-and-mouse game with the traffickers. If the traffickers discovered my true reason for being in Sapa, it could be dangerous not only for Marinho and me, but also for May.

I'd now understood Michael's emphasis on moving slowly and carefully, and was determined to act more cautiously in future.

Because so many girls had disappeared from May's group, I was certain there was someone in May's immediate circle – a friend, or even a family member – who had betrayed the girls to the traffickers. At least one of those people could not be trusted, and none of them was beyond suspicion.

Until I learned more, I'd have to be very careful speaking to anyone in that circle – but these were the same people I'd have to speak to, if I was to have any hope of identifying May's traffickers. These people had the clues I needed. I had to learn all I could about May's abduction, without revealing the reason for my curiosity.

I was in a position where, for the sake of my kidnapped friend, I'd have to deceive her own family and my other friends who remained in Sapa. Morally, it was an uncomfortable situation – but, practically speaking, there was a bigger problem.

Although my family was never particularly religious, I'd attended Sunday School as a child. While the religion itself had no lasting effect, I'd been left with a deep moral sense – in particular, I'd become a stickler for the truth.

It wasn't a helpful characteristic: my compulsive honesty had rarely brought me anything but trouble. People thought they wanted to hear the truth, until they heard it.

I hated lying and, on the rare occasion I deemed it necessary, I was such an awkward and unpracticed liar my deceit could be spotted from a mile away.

It was a character trait that had affected every aspect of my life. Because of my constant urge to tell the truth, I'd had to live a life which I could be comfortable telling the truth about. I held myself to a higher standard, even in situations that nobody was aware of, or was ever likely to know of.

I'd once read that the most intelligent and successful members of a society were also the most proficient liars, an idea which horrified me. I wanted to believe that it was possible to be both honest and successful – otherwise, I knew I was condemned to a life of failure.

Now, not only was I hunting for the truth in a small town of secrets and lies, I was in a position where I'd have to consistently deceive all of my local friends for a period of weeks or even months. The safety – and perhaps even the lives – of myself and others depended on it.

I was the worst possible candidate for such a job, and knew there was no way I could maintain a lie on such a grand scale. I'd ruin everything at the first opportunity.

My only realistic option was to lie by omission – to tell a story that was true, but wasn't the whole truth – and hope that nobody asked me any awkward questions.

Marinho and I had first begun working together in Indonesia, four months earlier. To help raise awareness of the global human trafficking crisis, we'd undertaken a gruelling overland search for 99 local people I'd photographed on my first journey through Asia, several years earlier.

We still hadn't finished that search: Marinho and I were yet to search for more of those people in Cambodia, China, Nepal, and India.

While that longer journey had been expensive and exhausting, it now gave Marinho and me an ideal cover story for our work in Sapa.

When we sat down for meals with my friends, we had plenty to talk about without ever mentioning our search for May. I spoke about our travels, and the people we'd already found. I recounted the stories, and showed them the photographs.

Amongst my collection of 99 portraits, there were eight faces from the Sapa region. Over the following weeks, while Marinho and I covertly investigated May's disappearance, we openly searched for and found all eight of those people.

That search justified our presence in Sapa, but not my investigation. I'd be asking all kinds of questions about my friends' abductions and would be recording the answers, preferably on camera. I couldn't write it off as mere curiosity – could I?

I began to formulate a plan. Gradually – over a period of several weeks, so as not to raise suspicion – I'd arrange to meet my Hmong friends, alone or in pairs. I'd tell them I was making a video about the Hmong people in Sapa – which was true, even if it wasn't the whole truth.

I'd arrange a room where we could speak privately, and Marinho would set up the cameras. I'd keep the atmosphere casual, beginning with a series of vague and innocent questions.

I'd ask the girls about their brothers and sisters, and the villages where they'd been born. I'd ask them which crops their families grew, and what kinds of animals they owned. I'd ask them about local beliefs and customs, and their own lives peddling handicrafts to tourists.

I'd let the conversation meander. Eventually, inevitably, it would turn to the elephant in the room: the disappearances of our mutual friends. Without seeming too eager, I'd gently pursue the subject, and the real interview would begin.

The cameras, which might have seemed a little intimidating at first, would soon be forgotten. Ultimately, they'd provide a more accurate and less intrusive record than taking notes. Instead of madly jotting down details, I could pretend I was only vaguely curious, so as not to arouse the girls' suspicions.

When I'd found out as much as I could about the abductions, I'd let the interview drift back to other subjects, and trail off into casual conversation. I'd get the information I needed – on camera, in a controlled environment – while leaving my friends unaware of my true purpose.

At a later date, when it seemed safe to do so, I would tell the girls the truth about my work. I didn't want to use their interviews for our documentary unless they had a clear understanding of what I was doing, and were entirely comfortable with their own participation.

I'd update Michael and my brother Nick regularly throughout the investigation, to explain who I was meeting with, what I had learned, and my understanding of the situation as it evolved. If for any reason they lost contact with Marinho and me, they'd be able to pick up the pieces and find out what had happened to us.

That was my plan, and I believed it was a good one – but it fell apart almost immediately, within the first minutes of my very first meeting.

CONFUSION IN THE MARKETPLACE

My first days in Sapa brought an unexpected challenge: I no longer knew where to find my Hmong friends.

I'd never had to contact any of the girls before – they'd always just been there on the corner of the street. Now the corner was empty, and my friends were nowhere to be seen.

I'd never had a phone in Sapa, so I'd never asked for their numbers. I'd helped many of the girls set up their first Facebook accounts, and we were still connected there – but their literacy levels were low, they didn't check their messages often, and I knew it wouldn't be easy to arrange a rendezvous.

I couldn't ask for my friends by name: there were dozens of girls in Sapa named Zao, or Vu, or Chu. I wasn't sure I could describe them very well, either – the last time I'd seen them, the girls had been partway through puberty, and would certainly have changed since then.

My friends had lived in small rented rooms in Sapa, but I'd only ever been there to help them move, and couldn't remember the exact locations.

Most of the girls came from the same village, a half-hour motorbike ride from Sapa – but the village sprawled across the lower slopes of a mountain, with no clear central point. I'd never visited their homes and families, and wasn't sure where to start looking.

In any case, I didn't know if my friends could even be found in Sapa, or at their family homes. While I still thought of them as girls, my Hmong friends were now in their late teens, and had grown into young women. Some of them must have already married, and would now be living with their husbands in other villages.

It was a laughable situation: how could I ever hope to find May in the immensity of China, if I couldn't even find my friends in the small town I'd once called home?

The girls were not the only ones to have grown. In the past three and a half years, Sapa itself had expanded. A profusion of new hotels and restaurants were now stretching skyward. Charlie's – the café that my friend Toan and I had opened together – was gone, its murals long since painted over. It had become a clothing shop, indistinguishable from a dozen others in Sapa. The grassy square in the centre of town was now paved, and the market there had been shut down.

The young Hmong women who had once thronged the streets selling handicrafts to tourists had all but vanished. Many had taken refuge against the bitterly cold January weather. Many others, I learned, had been kidnapped and sold in China.

As I wandered through the town, memories from my final days in Sapa came back to me. Each memory was anchored in a precise location: talking to May and her friends on the steps where they used to sit, the bench by the lake where we'd taken photos together, the corner where I'd left the girls after my farewell party, the paved area near Charlie's where May had given me her parting gifts.

All of these places were now cold and empty, inhabited only by the ghosts of memory.

I was delighted to find that the local market, off Cau May Street, had hardly changed at all. Those dimly-lit spaces between rows of concrete pillars formed the chambers of Sapa's beating heart. The villagers – the lifeblood of Sapa, in their costumes of the brightest red and deepest blue – circulated through the streets, but were inevitably drawn back there.

While the frigid winter weather had slowed the market's pulse, the beat remained just as I'd remembered it.

There at the market, the girls who hawked their handicrafts and the tourists they chased through the streets could set aside their roles. They sat shoulder-to-shoulder along the crude wooden benches, sharing the same simple meals, chatting in a babel of languages both local and foreign.

Marinho and I were sometimes invited to eat with Toan and Huong's family at the Yellow Dragon hotel, where I'd previously lived and worked. At other times we ate in the small restaurants that lined Sapa's streets, but we took most of our meals at the market. The food was cheap and delicious, and it was the best place in town to connect with the locals.

Our fourth day in Sapa was a Sunday – market day. Every Sunday, the villagers would put on their best clothing and come to Sapa to buy, sell, and socialise. For the first time since my return, the market was humming with life, and – at last – I saw a familiar face there.

Now in her late teens, Chu had grown taller, but seemed otherwise unchanged from the sweet, serious girl I'd known. She smiled and waved from across the market, and beckoned me to join her.

Chu was sitting with another Hmong girl named Chan. Chan was smaller and more animated, with a warm smile and bright, intelligent eyes.

Chu was surprised to learn that Chan and I didn't already know each other. She insisted that Chan had been one of the original members of May's group. Later, when I reconnected with other girls from that group, they all said the same thing.

Bizarrely, I had no recollection of Chan whatsoever. I couldn't remember seeing her face or even hearing her name, and I didn't know anything about her.

Nor could Chan remember having met me – yet she knew all about me. Right there in the middle of the bustling marketplace, Chan began talking about my work against human trafficking, and my true reason for having come back to Sapa.

All of the things I'd wanted to keep secret were suddenly being shared, in Sapa's most public place, by someone I'd barely met.

How did Chan know so much about me?

MOVIN' ON UP

Since my return to Sapa, I'd found myself living a strange double life.

On one hand, I was working to maintain absolute secrecy about my investigation into May's disappearance. On the other hand, our website explained exactly what I was doing and why. In preparation for the fundraising campaign we'd be launching the following week, an international team had begun spreading our message online, as far and wide as possible.

The fundraising campaign had originally been planned so that it would end before Marinho and I arrived in Sapa. As the campaign had been delayed by a month and we'd come to Sapa much earlier than expected, however, the heavily-promoted campaign and my highly-secretive investigation were both taking place at the same time.

It was an awkward situation, and one I would have otherwise avoided, but we desperately needed the funding.

As a precaution, we didn't refer to May or Sapa by name in any of our work, and the only photograph I'd shared of May was heavily pixellated. We'd set up our website so that anyone trying to access it from within Vietnam or China would be redirected to a dummy version of the site, which made no mention of human trafficking. While it wouldn't stop a more sophisticated user from uncovering the truth, it would fool the vast majority of people.

It was extremely unlikely that Chan, or any of the other local people in Sapa, had accessed our real website.

The missing piece of the puzzle was a Swiss man named Davide. Davide had been a friend of May's, and was now following my work. He had also married Chan's elder sister, who lived with him in Europe.

Davide knew I'd returned to Sapa to investigate May's abduction. He'd told Chan to keep an eye out for me, and encouraged her to help me if she could.

As it happened, Chan needed very little encouragement. She fully supported my work and, over the coming months, went to great lengths to assist me. She arranged meetings, interpreted for me, and explained some of the finer points of Hmong culture.

Not only did Chan become my greatest ally in Sapa, she also became a close friend, and all that I did there would have been impossible without her.

Chu and Chan were among the most intelligent and forward-thinking Hmong people I'd met in Sapa. Disciplined and hard-working, they both had a remarkable capacity for seeing the bigger picture, and for planning long-term.

They were the only two girls from their group of ten to have finished high school. Because of their studies, they'd had less time to sell handicrafts, or to guide tourists to the outlying villages. They'd done so only on weekends, and sometimes in the afternoons.

Even so, Chan had worked hard and saved an incredible amount of money by local standards. By the time I met her, at the age of nineteen, she'd already bought a well-sited plot of land and enough quality timber to build her own home in the village.

It's impossible to overstate what a phenomenal accomplishment this was for a Hmong woman in Sapa. I'd hoped that May and her friends would find a way to take advantage of the opportunities unfolding around them, and to break free from the cultural bonds that held them down – and here I saw it actually happening.

It was an achievement that would radically alter all aspects of Chan's life, and give younger girls a role model to aspire to. If and when Chan chose to marry, she would do so on her own terms – not as a dependent in her husband's home, but as a landowner and the mistress of her own household.

Meanwhile, Chu was the only girl of the group to pursue a university education; she aspired to a steady, well-paid job in healthcare. Once she had finished her studies, I had little doubt that Chu would also meet life on her own terms.

For all their success, Chu and Chan were both very modest, and generous with their time. I had enormous respect and admiration for them both.

While other young women their age had taken to wearing the more convenient and fashionable Western clothing, I was glad to see that Chu and Chan still wore the traditional Hmong costumes. Perhaps it was only for the sake of winning favour from tourists, who they still took trekking to the villages, but I hoped it was something more than that.

I hoped it was a sign that these intelligent young women weren't leaving their community behind – that they were bringing it with them, towards a brighter future.

LOST AND RUNNING

There was no longer any need for secrecy with Chu and Chan. They had my full trust – and, in any case, they already knew the essential facts of my work.

Chu and Chan hadn't yet made plans for the day, and agreed immediately to an interview. We relocated to a private room where we could speak freely, and Marinho arranged the cameras and microphones.

The girls knew just how devastating human trafficking could be. Not only had the traffickers taken five girls from their group of ten, but Chan's elder sister had also been kidnapped some years earlier. Hers was a fascinating story which showed how clever and courageous the Hmong girls could be, and I'll tell it here as Chan told it to me.

Chan's sister had begun chatting with two young Hmong men online. They told her they were Vietnamese

Hmong from a village near Lao Cai, the nearby border crossing to China.

Only much later did she learn that they were in fact Chinese Hmong and had no interest in her friendship, but were planning to kidnap and sell her.

The two young men came to Sapa to meet with Chan's sister and her cousin. Together, they rented two motorbikes to visit the Silver Waterfall, a half-hour ride from Sapa. Chan's sister rode on the back of one bike, Chan's cousin on the back of the other.

After seeing the waterfall, the young men persuaded the girls to come and see their village, which they claimed was an hour's ride from Sapa. They'd have to be back in Sapa before nightfall to return the rented motorbikes, but it was still morning, and there was plenty of time.

On the way to the village, the two motorbikes separated, and the girls lost sight of each other. After a time, Chan's sister found herself riding beside a river, on a road that was unfamiliar to her. She began to see signs written in Chinese.

She asked the man where he was taking her, and why they were in China. He insisted that they were still in Vietnam, on the way to his village. It was then that she realised he'd been lying to her, and that something was terribly wrong.

Chan's sister was alone and helpless in a foreign country. She considered jumping from the moving motorbike and trying to run away, but she was afraid that she'd be injured, which would only leave her more vulnerable.

I remembered the teenage girl I'd once seen lying on the road in northern Thailand, and how terrifying it must have been for her to leap from a moving motorbike.

Chan's sister had another idea. She wriggled up as close as she could to the man in front of her, put her arm around him – and snatched the key from the ignition.

The bike stopped dead. Chan's sister jumped off and leaped away, refusing to surrender the key. She told the man to call his friend, to tell him to bring her cousin there. She refused to go anywhere unless they all went together.

The man did as he was told: he called his friend, who brought Chan's cousin there to meet them.

By this time it was clear that the girls had been kidnapped, and they were certain that the two men were planning to sell them.

From their work with tourists, the two girls had learned to speak English, and the men spoke none. The girls spoke together in English and decided to run away, to try to find their own way home.

It seems that Chan's sister threw the key into some bushes, forcing the men to search for it. While they were distracted, Chan's sister and cousin ran down to the river, and hid amongst the reeds.

The men hadn't seen where the girls had gone, but knew they were somewhere along the river. They took a long stick and started walking along the bank, poking around in the reeds and water for a long time. They came close to where the girls were hiding, and very nearly prodded Chan's sister with the stick – but the girls were lucky, and the men passed by without seeing them.

In the end, the young men decided to let the girls go. Their morning in Vietnam had still been a profitable one – they had the two motorbikes, which they could sell in China. They got back on the bikes and rode away.

Chan's sister and cousin didn't know where they were, or how to get back to Sapa. They spent the rest of the day walking through the forested mountains, uncertain if the paths were leading them back towards Vietnam or only deeper into China.

Dusk fell, and they became lost in the darkening forest.

It was after midnight when the two girls finally crossed back into Vietnam, close to Lao Cai. They came to a place Chan's sister recognised, and she called her parents to come and pick them up.

By that time, the Vietnamese police were looking for the girls – not because they were missing, but because the man who owned the rental company had reported his motorbikes stolen.

The girls were taken to the police station in Sapa and said they'd been kidnapped, but the police refused to believe them. They were ordered to pay for the motorbikes – a significant sum for young Hmong women, and a poor welcome home after all they'd been through.

Chan's sister had the phone number of the young man who'd kidnapped her, and was determined to catch him. At four o'clock that morning, instead of going home to rest, she went back to a certain place on the border near Lao Cai. She called the man and told her she needed his help to get home, begging him to come and pick her up.

Perhaps sensing a trap, the man refused. Chan's sister spent the whole day there trying to convince him, but he didn't dare come back across the border.

Chan's sister didn't give up. She crossed the border herself, approached the Chinese police, and paid them to catch the two men. Sadly, I learned that this was the reality on both sides of the border: if you expected the police to act, they would often expect something in return.

Using the information Chan's sister gave them, the Chinese police caught the first man, but not his friend.

They questioned the man, asking how many girls he'd trafficked into China. After insisting it was his first time, he ultimately confessed to kidnapping three other girls. He didn't know what had become of them after he'd sold them across the border.

The trafficker was imprisoned, and his family was ordered to pay for the motorbike.

At that time, more and more girls were beginning to disappear from the area, and the Vietnamese police didn't know which routes the traffickers were using to cross the border. Chan's sister showed them the path her kidnapper had taken. The police began monitoring it, discovered it was a popular crossing for traffickers, and caught several others trying to cross there with kidnapped girls.

It was a rare thing: a human trafficking story with a positive ending. If not for the courage and quick-thinking of Chan's sister, the story would have ended very differently – and might never have been told at all.

Was there any hope that May's story might still have a positive ending? Would we ever find out what had happened to her?

THE MYSTERY

I interviewed Chu and Chan for the best part of two hours.

They were the ideal people to speak to about the local human trafficking crisis – clever young women who had a thorough understanding of the situation from the inside, as well as the judgement to see it more objectively.

They'd heard all of the stories from the girls who had returned from China, and had the intelligence to put the pieces together. They seemed to understand a great deal about how the trafficking networks operated – and, as I learned more over the following months, almost every word they said fit with my own observations.

The effect of human trafficking on Sapa had been devastating. The entire Sapa district – including the town itself and perhaps two dozen villages scattered across several broad valleys - had a total population of only around 55,000 people.

Chu and Chan told me that in just one year, a single village might lose twenty girls or more to human trafficking. While there were no reliable statistics, it was clear that a hundred girls or more – likely many more – were being taken from the district every year. With each passing year, the number continued to rise.

And Sapa was not the hardest-hit region: there were villages closer to the border which were suffering even greater losses.

Most of the trafficked girls never came home, and many were never heard from again. For the fortunate few who were able to escape and return home, life would never be the same.

From Chu and Chan's group, five girls had been kidnapped – my friends May, Pang, and Vu, plus May's sister Cho and a fifth girl named Shu.

Cho's story was an extremely strange one. While I was yet to understand her situation, Cho was now in contact with her parents, and she didn't seem to need or want any assistance.

Vu and Shu had already returned home from China, and so I focused my investigation on May and Pang, who were still missing.

Pang's case seemed to have been a typical one – a young Hmong man from out of town had courted her for several weeks, until one day they'd both vanished from Sapa. Chu and Chan had seen them together, and they had a reasonable recollection of what the man looked like, but had never seen him again.

May's abduction, however, was more of a mystery.

The best information I had about May's abduction had come from May's English friend Laura, who had been living in Hanoi and had made her own enquiries at the time of May's disappearance.

Laura had told me that May had been planning to attend school in Hanoi together with an unnamed female friend.

It was a hospitality school, I learned – and that friend was Chan.

In the weeks before May's abduction in mid-2011, May and Chan had been spending a great deal of time with each other. They'd been planning to leave Sapa and travel to the school together, but May had changed her mind at the last moment.

According to the story Laura had been told, May's father had fallen ill, and May had remained behind to help her family.

That was just a pretence, Chan said. The real reason for May's change of plans was because she'd had a boyfriend in Sapa, and she was reluctant to leave him.

And so Chan had gone to Hanoi by herself. May had stayed behind in Sapa, and had been kidnapped the very next day.

I assumed that May's abduction followed the usual pattern – that the boyfriend was from out of town, and had also disappeared from Sapa – but I was wrong.

May's boyfriend was from Sapa, and he was still there.

I was confused. What role had the boyfriend played in May's disappearance?

If he hadn't taken her, then who had – and how?

May's boyfriend was a young man named Chinh. Chu and Chan assured me that Chinh was a good man, who had genuinely loved May and had been devastated by her disappearance. Chu said that Chinh had called her in tears when he'd first learned that May was gone.

If May had already been in a loving relationship, how had another man gotten close enough to kidnap her?

May's trafficker remained a mystery to Chu and Chan. They didn't know who he was, or how he'd taken her.

"She just gone, we don't know," said Chan. "Never ever see her again."

DO YOU BELIEVE IN MAGIC

One of the people I most wanted to find in Sapa was Vu.

Vu might not have anything new to tell me about May and Pang's abductions, but she could certainly help me understand their current situations. Vu knew exactly how it felt to have been stolen from Sapa and sold into marriage in China.

Chu and Chan gave me her phone number, and she came to see me two days later.

Vu had grown from an awkward girl into an attractive young woman with a button nose, full lips, and black hair cascading halfway down her back.

Vu and I had never known each other particularly well, and she seemed to have had trust issues even before her trafficking – yet she fully supported my work, and understood its importance better than most.

It was surreal to think of everything Vu had experienced in the three and a half years since I'd last seen her. She'd been kidnapped, trafficked across an international border, and forced into marriage with a foreign stranger.

Two years earlier, though she'd never given him her number, a young Hmong man had begun calling Vu's phone. She'd soon realised that they had mutual friends and had even briefly met once.

The man began calling Vu every day, telling her she was beautiful, that he loved her, and that he wanted to marry her. He wasn't from Sapa, but kept offering to come back there to meet her again. He was very insistent, and wore her down gradually.

Vu finally agreed to meet him in Sapa's main square. They walked around the lake together, and sat down to talk. Vu didn't find the man attractive – in fact, she thought he was particularly ugly – but then something strange happened.

Vu says she began to lose control of her body. She could still see and hear what was happening around her, but her tongue felt as though it had frozen, and she lost the ability to speak. The young man who had seemed so ugly suddenly seemed very attractive to her.

The kidnappers had many kinds of dangerous medicines, Vu told me. Some made you fall asleep, or fall in love with them, or made you incapable of speaking.

I've since heard many stories of human trafficking victims being drugged in Sapa. In some cases, drugging seemed a plausible explanation for the events described. Perhaps a girl had been offered something to eat or drink, and said she'd felt drowsy or lost consciousness soon afterwards.

For many of the girls, however, there seemed to be a blurred line between medicine and magic. Vu believed that the medicine was a sticky paste, which the kidnapper would apply with his bare hands to his victim's hair or clothing. In her own case, she recalled the man touching her hair, and was certain that that's when she'd been drugged.

Even Chu and Chan, who didn't believe in magic as many Hmong people did, believed that the kidnappers often used some mysterious kind of medicine to make their victims follow them.

Perhaps the "medicine" really did exist – or perhaps it was just a pretext a victim could use to save face. She could use it to absolve herself of any perceived guilt or embarrassment, to explain away anything that might otherwise draw the condemnation of her community.

Girls who claimed to have been drugged often gave very different accounts of their kidnappings when compared to versions given by other witnesses. In the three months of my investigation in Sapa, nobody ever described seeing an unconscious or paralysed girl being placed on the back of a motorbike.

In a region where victims were so heavily shamed and blamed for their own abductions, it was easy to see why the girls might want to protect their reputations by any means possible. Claiming to have been drugged seemed like a common way for a survivor to salvage some respect in the wake of her return home.

I found myself facing a moral dilemma.

On one hand, I could understand and appreciate why it might be important for a survivor to take control of her own narrative, particularly in the face of such harsh criticism from her own community. I could hardly imagine the ordeals these girls and women had been through.

On the other hand, I was working to uncover the truth. Vu, and some of the other survivors I met, told me things that just didn't seem to make any sense. How was I to understand what really happened when there was so little objective evidence, and my only witness was seemingly unreliable?

Ultimately, I decided, my allegiance was to the truth.

I never challenged any of the survivors' accounts directly. Because I knew the girls personally, lived in the same town, and saw them reasonably often, I had the advantage of being able to revisit their stories at later dates.

With Vu, for example, I held two formal interviews followed by a series of casual conversations, which allowed me to unobtrusively double-check any details which didn't quite add up.

By covering the same ground two or three times over a period of several months, I could see which parts of the story stuck, and which parts changed. Sometimes

I heard alternate versions of the same stories which the survivors had previously told their friends, which also helped fill in some of the blanks.

I'd gather as much information as possible, and put together the most complete and accurate picture I could. It was like trying to assemble a jigsaw puzzle with many pieces missing, and plenty of others that didn't quite fit together.

Vu told me that, while she was drowsy or insensible, a second man appeared. The two men took her on a motorbike down to Lao Cai, then continued north into Muong Khuong province.

The "medicine" began to wear off and Vu gradually came to her senses, though she was still unable to speak. She considered jumping from the bike, but it was moving too quickly, and she was sandwiched between the two men.

They'd left Sapa in the afternoon, and it was already dark when they stopped by a river. Vu tried to run away, but the first man quickly caught her. He told her he was taking her home to marry her; then he picked her up and began carrying her. Vu's feet splashed in the water, and she realised she was being taken across the river into China.

For about an hour, Vu sat waiting with her kidnapper on the far side of the river. It was very dark, she said, and the man had already taken her phone. Another man came with a motorbike to pick them up. They were taken a short distance by bike, then spent the rest of the night travelling by bus.

Eventually, they arrived in what Vu described as a "big city" – but coming from a small town like Sapa, it's difficult to know exactly what she meant by this. Vu's kidnapper passed her to a Chinese Hmong couple, who took her in a second bus. The kidnapper left, and she never saw him again.

News of Vu's disappearance reached her mother, at home in their village, and she wept.

Several days later, Vu's mother went to her daughter's rented room in Sapa and emptied it out, taking Vu's clothing and bedding back to the village.

For reasons unknown, she never reported Vu's abduction to the Vietnamese authorities.

VIDEO GAMES

Vu spent only one night in the home of the Chinese Hmong couple. All she could remember was crying, and refusing to eat. The next day she changed hands, then changed hands again.

Vu was taken by two young Chinese Hmong middlemen. They took her to their home, where she remained for four or five days. The two men terrified her, for reasons she chose not to elaborate.

The middlemen called for demonstrations of Vu's domestic skills, and – not being an experienced cook – she struggled to prepare the dishes they demanded of her. Their dialect was very different to her own, but she could still understand much of what they said.

One day Vu heard them speaking about their elder brother, who had already been imprisoned for trafficking girls. He was to be released and would return home the following week.

Vu never saw him: by that time, she'd already been sold to the man who would become her "husband".

Chinese men came to the house to look at her. When one of the men offered to buy her, Vu was so desperate to get away from the middlemen that she went willingly.

The man lived in a distant part of China. They travelled there by sleeper bus, a journey which took "two or three nights".

Vu and the man who'd bought her spoke no common language.

"We are speaking like chicken and duck," she said. "We not understand each other."

I can only imagine Vu's incredible sense of isolation as she was being taken by this foreign stranger towards an unknown fate, ever further from the only home she'd ever known.

They took multiple buses, all full of Chinese people. Vu made no attempt to communicate with any of them – she was scared, couldn't speak their language, and was worried she'd only make her situation worse. Even if she could have escaped the man who'd bought her, she couldn't imagine how she would ever find her way back to Sapa.

She decided it would be better to go with the man, to stay with him awhile and learn to speak some Chinese, then try to find her way home.

And so Vu found herself living as the forced bride of a strange man in another country, and she hated it. Vu was perhaps fifteen years old when she'd been kidnapped. The man who'd bought her was a decade older, in his mid-twenties.

For the first two months after arriving at his home, Vu said she'd cried constantly. She didn't want to do anything, and often didn't want to eat.

Her "husband" was unemployed. They lived with his parents, and he spent his days playing video games. He'd sit at the computer from eight or nine o'clock in the morning until around midnight, sometimes later.

The man's family expected Vu to wash the clothes, clean the house, and tend to the vegetable garden. Sometimes she cooked. She wasn't allowed to leave the house and, when she wasn't busy with chores, Vu didn't know what to do with herself.

She was bored, and frequently angry with her "husband". She said they fought every day. When they were upset with each other, she'd lock herself in the bedroom and distract herself with Chinese TV.

Vu's "husband" wanted her to get a job, though he himself didn't seem to be looking for one. He also wanted Vu to have a baby. His main incentive seemed to be the money his father had promised him as a gift.

Vu didn't seem to have a choice in the matter – and, oddly, she didn't seem to have a strong opinion about it. If she'd married a Hmong man in Sapa, Vu wouldn't have been given that choice, and she had no reason to expect it now. While it would have been horrible to bear the child of a man she hated, perhaps she thought a baby might alleviate her boredom and loneliness.

After a time, Vu began to get used to her new life, and it no longer upset her as much as it had. Although she could speak very little, she began to understand some Chinese from watching TV. When she did try to speak, her pronunciation was very different to that of her "husband" - presumably she was learning standard Mandarin from the television, while her "husband" spoke with a local inflection.

One day Vu went to the market with her "husband" and his family, and saw a Western man there. She wanted to speak with him, to ask his help to get home to Sapa, but never had the chance.

The moment passed, and Vu went back to her new life, in her new home, with the man who called himself her husband.

WHITE WEDDING

When referring to Vu's "husband", I use inverted commas as a reminder that his "marriage" to Vu was not in any way legitimate.

How could it be? Their relationship – made possible only by a financial arrangement with a third party – was based on fear and coercion.

Vu was still a child, of perhaps fifteen years. She was being held in China against her will, had no legal status there, and no woman in China could be legally married until the age of twenty. Even if she had understood the language, Vu was in no position to give her consent.

The "marriage" was, essentially, a one-sided fantasy by a grown man and his family, into which they had forced an unwilling child. In no way does it deserve the respect given to the institution of marriage, only the horror and revulsion evoked by slavery, rape, and pedophilia.

Vu's "wedding" had not been formalised with any paperwork.

I was amazed to learn, however, that her "husband's" family and friends had all celebrated the "marriage" – and, incredibly, the entire event had been recorded on video by hired professionals.

I struggled to make sense of it. Why would anyone pay to record and publicise a crime they were committing? Was the trafficking of girls so common, and so socially acceptable in China? Had forcing a helpless child into an illegitimate marriage become a matter of pride, rather than shame?

I couldn't imagine how surreal Vu's "wedding" must have been – but I didn't have to. Among the very few possessions Vu had taken with her when she'd escaped China was a copy of her wedding DVD, which she offered to share with me.

She'd had an album of wedding photos in China, which she'd also wanted to bring home, but it had been too big for her to carry. Vu had stolen her "husband's" phone when she'd escaped China, and it had also contained many of their wedding photos, but she said her friend had accidentally erased them all when fumbling through the Chinese-language menus.

The "wedding" had taken place in the final week of March 2012, several weeks after Vu had arrived at her "husband's" house.

The DVD was poorly produced, with tacky

computer-generated animations and kitschy video effects. Relentlessly upbeat Chinese pop songs were intercut with melodramatic instrumentals.

"We're happy that destiny brought us together," proclaimed the opening title, in Chinese characters.

The "wedding" itself – as a modern Chinese wedding – combined both Chinese and Western traditions. Vu wore a white wedding dress, for example. A Chinese bride would have traditionally worn red, the colour of luck and happiness, rather than white, which is associated with death and mourning.

In this case, however, the symbolism seemed fitting.

Vu described how she'd been dolled up in a fancy dress, make-up, and high heels. It was the first time she'd ever worn heels, she said, and it was "scary".

When she appeared onscreen, Vu looked beautiful in her long shoulderless wedding dress, with her glittering necklace, tiara, and train. The man who'd bought her, on the other hand, was a remarkably unattractive man with a sour expression on his sallow, cratered face. He wore a baggy, ill-fitting grey suit with a blue striped tie, and he seemed uncomfortable on camera.

The video showed his family home – a compact, two-storey building with an enclosed yard, in a semi-rural area. Dozens of pink banknotes had been pinned to a large red wall-hanging in the shape of the double-happiness symbol, a common motif at Chinese weddings. A group of working-class people in street clothes – mostly men – sat hunched over a table, smoking cigarettes and drinking tea out of plastic cups.

It was a sunny day, but the guests were dressed warmly against the cold. They shot off firecrackers in the laneway beside the house, then piled into a series of silver and black vehicles. The "groom" rode in a gleaming black Audi 4WD, festooned with flowers and pink ribbons.

For a family that did not seem wealthy, I imagined that buying Vu and paying for the "wedding" would have come at considerable expense.

There was a long sequence showing the convoy entering a large city, before pulling into a carpark beside a line of shops.

Traditionally, a groom would collect his bride from her father's house, after paying respect to her family. In this case, ironically enough, Vu's "husband" simply picked her up from a shop, which seemed to be a photography studio.

Vu was shown sitting inside, smiling uncomfortably, not seeming to know exactly what was expected of her. The "groom" presented her with a bouquet of pink roses, pinned one to her chest, and pretended to kiss her cheek for the sake of the camera.

Outside, the "groom" seemed to be almost dragging Vu along as he led her back to the car. Even in her high heels, Vu barely reached his shoulder. Another long montage followed the convoy back to his house.

More guests had joined the celebrations, including children and teenagers. They sat and drank soft drink, while women carried bowls of food from the kitchen.

There didn't seem to be any exchange of vows – but how could there be, when Vu spoke no Chinese?

Vu had no family or friends at the "wedding", of course, and she couldn't communicate with anyone around her. I wondered if the other guests were curious about this mystery bride. How did Vu's "husband" feel about buying a teenage wife – and how did Vu herself feel?

There was one shot on the DVD I found particularly unsettling. Vu was sitting alone in the backseat of the 4WD outside her "husband's" house, and she looked terrified.

I remembered Vu saying she'd cried constantly for the first two months with her "husband". I had no doubt that Vu's "marriage" had been a terrible, deeply traumatic time in her life – and yet, as the video showed, her experience had been far more complex than that.

The first part of the DVD showed a series of still photographs from a professional studio session. Vu and her "husband" appeared in a variety of outfits and poses – their hands touching, her head on his shoulder, his arms around her waist. She held a large lollypop, and he clasped a stuffed toy.

In many of the photographs, Vu's smile looked forced, and at other times it was barely a smile at all – but sometimes, her smile did actually seem genuine.

The strangest part of the video, though, was five minutes of awkwardly-staged footage where Vu and her "husband" pretended to be in love. No doubt this was a standard part of the filmmaker's package – an intimate sequence showing the couple alone and relaxed together, revealing the romance beyond the rituals.

In the case of Vu and her "husband", however, it only highlighted how very little they knew each other, and how uncomfortable they were in each other's presence. It was abundantly clear that they were two strangers in an absurdly forced situation.

This segment had been recorded on a cold, windy day in a large public garden. The trees were still mostly bare after the winter, and there didn't seem to be anyone else around.

Vu's "husband" stood with a rose clenched in his teeth, while Vu looked down at the ground. He pushed her on a swing, and they tottered together on a see-saw. They walked slowly between the trees, crouched on the grass, and sat awkwardly on a bench. Vu's "husband" stood behind her with his hands on her waist while she slowly flapped her arms like a bird. They feigned interest in a tree, a rose petal, and a lantern. Each of them curved an arm above their head to form one-half of a badly misshapen love-heart. They looked into each other's eyes, gazed off into the distance, and stared straight at the camera. They held hands, and paced around in circles.

I could imagine the filmmaker directing them through this ludicrous series of poses, struggling to spark a little warmth between this couple that seemed almost as cold as the weather.

As I watched the DVD, I tried to understand how Vu must have been feeling.

Just a few weeks earlier, she'd been with her family and friends in Sapa. Now she was in a foreign country, not only being forced to marry a stranger, but to pretend that she was happy about it.

The strangest part of all was that sometimes, Vu did actually seem happy.

NOTHING BETTER

Vu had been sold into marriage in China.

To the Western mind, that's shocking – but in many parts of Asia, it's perfectly normal. Even at home in Sapa, Vu would have been sold into marriage.

When a Hmong girl marries, her father doesn't give her away: he sells her – for money, meat, and alcohol. She then belongs to her husband's family. If she wants a divorce and her birth family is willing to take her back, they'll negotiate a partial refund with her husband's family.

A few days after our first interview with Vu, Marinho and I were invited to a wedding in one of the villages outside Sapa. The venue was a typical Hmong dwelling – small, dark, and crudely built, with three rooms and a loft above.

The central room was also the largest, with a bare

concrete floor and gaps in the walls. There was a rudimentary altar facing the main door – squares of coloured paper stuck to the wall, with sticks of incense standing in a small wooden box beneath.

To the right of the altar was a small damp room with a smoky fire in the middle of the floor, and to the left was a primitive kitchen. Here, the leg and hindquarter of a pig were strung up on the wall, the raw flesh exposed. The pig's face and skin hung beside them. A buffalo's leg stuck out of a carrying basket, hoof and all, its skin stripped off above the hairy ankle.

A Hmong wedding lasts for two days: the first day is held at the house of the bride's father, and the next at the house of the groom's family. In the small dark room to the right of the altar, Marinho and I witnessed the most important moment of the entire wedding. It wasn't the vows, or a kiss – the bride wasn't even there.

It was a cool January morning and the men gathered around the fire, wrapped in their jackets. They took turns smoking tobacco from a thick bamboo water-pipe, then poured and drank several shots of rice wine from a curved black buffalo horn.

A rattan tray was placed on the bare concrete floor. One of the men took out of his jacket a small package folded in a sheet of plain white paper. The paper was opened to reveal a thick wad of brightly-coloured banknotes. This was the money the bride's father was being paid in exchange for his daughter.

The men from both families counted the money,

stacking it in piles on the tray, jabbing at each pile with their gnarled fingers. When at last they were satisfied that full payment had been made, they poured and drank again from the buffalo horn.

The father of the bride had just sold his daughter. Bundling up the money, he tucked it away in his jacket. Culturally speaking, the most crucial difference with Vu's "wedding" was that the money had been taken by her traffickers, and not by her father.

In Sapa, a father could ask any price he liked for his daughter. Some of the more progressive families weren't interested in profiting by the sale. They might ask only a token amount – perhaps six million dong (about $285).

However, these families were in the minority, and the average bride price in Sapa seemed to be increasing. In recent years, some fathers had been demanding as much as sixty million dong (around $2,850). This was a substantial sum of money for the villagers: with the same amount of money, a family could buy two fully-grown buffaloes.

Chan had a more progressive attitude, but believed that a bride price was still necessary. If your daughter was being married and you didn't ask for payment, she said, people would become suspicious and assume there was something wrong with her.

"People [would] say, 'Oh, this girl is no good, that's why her family give her for free'."

The transaction that Marinho and I had witnessed wasn't a purely financial one. Also included in the deal were twenty or twenty-five litres of rice wine, delivered in used soft drink bottles, and the large pig whose remains I'd seen in the kitchen. These were to be consumed at the wedding feast, which took place a short time later.

A wooden table had been set up in the central room of the house, but there wasn't enough space inside for all of the guests. A crude array of planks, low to the ground, were used for tables and benches in the yard outside the house. In some places, banana leaves were laid out as tablecloths.

Dozens of people crowded around steaming bowls of pork, potato, tofu, green vegetables, and broth. Rice was ladled out from battered pots, and a plastic tub of congealed blood was passed from hand to hand.

The central table was occupied predominantly by men – and, of the handful of women there, it was difficult to tell which was the bride. She wore the same traditional costume as the rest, and carried no bouquet of flowers. She certainly hadn't arrived in a limousine – there were no roads that reached so high up the mountain. The narrow, slippery trails here were accessible only by foot and motorbike.

The bride's father played a larger role in the wedding than the bride herself: she was merely part of the transaction.

It wasn't necessarily a happy day for the bride – she was leaving her family home for another village, to live with a man who might have been little more than a stranger to her. She would soon have to take on the responsibilities of marriage and motherhood, shouldering new burdens at home and in the fields.

There were high levels of alcohol abuse and domestic violence in the villages outside Sapa, and very few of the local men received any formal education to speak of. There was no saying how the bride might be treated by her husband.

For her sake, I hoped it wasn't the happiest day of her life.

Vu confirmed my suspicions, that she'd had mixed feelings about her "marriage" in China. By Western standards, her "wedding" had been a simple affair – but it was far more than she could have hoped for in Sapa. I could understand why she'd felt conflicted.

In Sapa, Vu had never been anyone special. She'd been ignored and overlooked, clinging to the fringes of May's group. Suddenly, in China, she'd become the centre of attention. In a stunning white dress and make-up, being chauffeured through the streets in a sleek black Audi, with filmmakers and photographers capturing her every move, she must have felt like a major celebrity.

Vu's wedding DVD showed the room she had shared with her "husband". It was a clean, well-lit room with freshly painted walls, glass windows, air conditioning, and a flatscreen TV. There was a couch, a desk, and a large, comfortable-looking bed.

While none of these things would be remarkable in the West, they simply didn't exist in Vu's village. She'd entered a new world she could have only dreamed of at home. Her prison was also a palace.

On one hand, Vu had been disconnected from everything she'd known in Vietnam – her family, friends, culture, language, and the land she knew. On the other hand, she'd had to work less, had been given far more material comfort, and had been expected to bear fewer children.

Being sold into marriage to an unknown and unpleasant man, while far from ideal, could very easily have happened to Vu in Sapa, too.

I was beginning to realise that my investigation wouldn't be nearly as simple as I'd hoped. I wondered what kind of lives May and Pang were living in China, and if Vietnam had anything left to offer them.

Even if I could find them, would they actually want to come home?

RUNAWAY

Despite the hardships of life in Sapa and the material comforts she'd been given in China, Vu had still been desperate to come home.

More than anything, she'd wanted to find a way to contact her aunt, a woman I knew as Big Zao. Vu was certain that Big Zao could help her.

Big Zao had also been kidnapped and forced into marriage in a distant part of China, and had escaped several years earlier. Hers was an inspirational story, which she later told me in person. She'd been kidnapped in mid-2008 – much earlier than anyone else I knew in Sapa.

Big Zao was still a teenager when she'd escaped her "husband". She'd succeeded in crossing China and returning home by herself, while six months pregnant.

I met Big Zao in her home. She was unusually tall

for a Hmong woman, with a warm smile, long golden earrings, and a nervous twitch which kept her blinking almost continuously. At that time, she was still in her early twenties – yet she spoke of her trafficking as if it were ancient history. It was a sharp reminder how incredibly young the Hmong girls were when they were kidnapped.

Six years earlier, two young Hmong men had come to Sapa and befriended Big Zao. They were several years older and had claimed to be from Muong Kuong province, in the borderlands to the north.

One of the men had offered to take Big Zao for a ride on his motorbike. He said they could go and visit his uncle in China, and come back the next day. Big Zao had no reason to be suspicious, and she went willingly.

The man took her to the house of a Hmong family across the border and left her there, telling her he'd come back soon.

When he didn't return, the family said he'd been in a near-fatal motorbike accident and had been taken to hospital. She was to wait with the family while he recovered. Big Zao felt awful, and eagerly awaited further news. It was two weeks before the family told her they had in fact bought her, and the man was never coming back.

Until that moment, Big Zao hadn't even suspected that she'd been trafficked. Her experience showed just how quickly and how dramatically the situation in Sapa had changed. By the time of my investigation, if a girl was missing even just for a few hours, it was often assumed immediately that she'd been trafficked to China.

Big Zao had been sold to a second Hmong family, and then a third. Each time, it seems she was taken deeper into China. She found herself held captive in a house with another girl, who had been kidnapped from a different Vietnamese province by a different man.

The girls were told they'd have to marry Chinese men, who began coming to the house to see them. Big Zao was made to feel that she was a burden on the Hmong family. She agreed to go with one of the men because she didn't want to impose herself on them any longer than necessary.

The fact that Big Zao was so considerate to her traffickers suggests that, even at that stage, she still hadn't fully understood her position. That seemed strange to me: Big Zao struck me as an otherwise intelligent woman.

The only explanation I can find is that Big Zao had been taken so far from anything she'd experienced, or even imagined, that she simply didn't know how to respond. As a Hmong girl raised in a very traditional society, and a gentle soul by nature, perhaps she hadn't yet considered doing any other than what she was told.

The man who bought Big Zao took her away by bus. He lived with his family in Guangdong province, in southeastern China. It took two days and a night to reach their village, and then the family had celebrated their "wedding".

The man wanted a child, and Big Zao soon fell pregnant. It made no difference to her whether she gave birth to a son or daughter – "but if I have a boy," she told me, "the daddy more happy. The daddy more like the boy."

Occasionally, when Big Zao's "husband" left for work, he'd leave her a little spending money. She was free to go to the village market and buy whatever she liked – but the only thing she wanted was to find her way home.

"Every day, every night, I thinking I want to come back to Vietnam only," she told me. "I miss a lot of friends in Vietnam. I miss my friends, my family."

Big Zao began collecting the money and hiding it away. After eight months, she said she had five hundred yuan (about $75), and hoped it would be enough for the journey back to Vietnam.

It wasn't much money, and it was a long way home, but Big Zao was determined to leave China before her child was born. If she gave birth in China, she was afraid she'd be stuck there for the rest of her life, and that was a possibility she refused to consider.

The nearest town was forty minutes away by bus. Big's Zao's "husband" had once taken her there, and she remembered where they'd gone to catch the bus. During the journey, she'd asked him where they were going, and hadn't forgotten the name he'd told her.

One day, when her "husband" was at work, Big Zao left the house. She found the bus stop, and the bus, and made her way into the town. She remembered the name of the city where her "husband" had bought her, and knew it was much closer to Vietnam.

By that time, Big Zao could understand some Chinese, but could speak very little. She spoke some English, but nobody seemed to understand it where she was.

She asked for help, in a mixture of Chinese and English. The people at the bus station were kind to her, helping her to buy a ticket and find the bus.

When she arrived at her destination, she didn't know where to go. She found her way to the market, where there were many Chinese Hmong people. One of them helped her to find the train station, where there was a Hmong woman behind the counter.

Big Zao told the Hmong woman that she was trying to get home to Vietnam, but the woman told her it was impossible. She said she had a friend who lived nearby, and that Big Zao could stay with her. In another year, perhaps, Big Zao would be able to speak enough Chinese to find her way home.

It's difficult to say whether the woman was genuinely trying to help Big Zao, or to trick her into being trafficked again. Big Zao and her unborn baby both had value on the black market, and could easily have been resold.

Big Zao rejected the woman's offer. The woman told her that her only other option was to spend the night in the train station, and the police would come and take her the next day.

With no legal status in China, Big Zao had no idea how the police might treat her. She was in a foreign country with no paperwork, she couldn't speak the language, and she couldn't guess what the police might do. I've since heard stories of trafficked girls being imprisoned for months in squalid conditions – and even re-trafficked – by the Chinese police.

It was a gamble, but Big Zao decided to take it.

HOMEWARD BOUND

The next morning, two police officers arrived at the station. One was Han – China's dominant ethnic group – and the other was Hmong.

The two officers took Big Zao in their car and drove for six hours. They said they were taking her in the direction of Vietnam, and Big Zao had no way of knowing otherwise. The three of them eventually reached another city, which was still a very long way from the border.

Bizarrely, the policemen then just left her there, and went back the way they'd come. They didn't hand her over to the local authorities, nor did they give her any paperwork to make her journey easier. They took her to a bus station, helped her buy a ticket, and left.

Big Zao kept going, inching ever closer to the border. She took another three-hour bus ride, spent another night in another strange city, and took a five-hour bus ride the next day.

I can only imagine how scared and exhausted Big Zao must have felt, as she watched her meagre savings rapidly disappearing.

Guangdong province, at its closest point, is a thousand kilometres by road from Sapa. Its furthest point is nearly two thousand kilometres away. China is not an especially cheap country to travel in, and Big Zao seemed to take a convoluted route back to the border. Five hundred yuan doesn't seem nearly enough to cover the costs of such a long journey. I wonder if there was some error in the figure Big Zao remembered, or if – somewhere along the way – she'd received some extra money from well-wishing strangers.

Big Zao had crossed China, but she still had to cross the border to reach Vietnam.

For the local people, the most formidable obstacle is not the border itself, but a line of checkpoints several kilometres inside the border, where the Chinese authorities check the identity cards of anyone passing through.

The traffickers knew how to avoid these checkpoints when taking girls into China. The few girls who were able to run away and reach the border region on their own, however, didn't know about the checkpoints or how to pass them. Getting through seemed to be a matter of luck, as much as anything, and anyone who failed to pass risked being detained indefinitely.

When the officers saw that Big Zao didn't have an identity card, they told her to get off the bus and follow them into their office. There was another girl there without an identity card, who was apparently in a very similar situation – it seemed she was also from one of Vietnam's minority groups, and was trying to go home.

The officers began questioning Big Zao. They wanted to know who she was, where she'd come from, and where she was going. They checked her ticket, and asked the bus driver about her.

Big Zao decided her best chance was to keep her mouth shut, and pretend not to understand their questions. Eventually the officers became frustrated with her, and simply let her go.

The other girl could speak more Chinese, and was still struggling to talk her way through when Big Zao was finally released. Big Zao had no way of knowing what had happened to her.

At last, Big Zao reached Hekou – the Chinese city that stood across the river from Lao Cai, an hour's journey from Sapa. This was a major border crossing with Vietnam, but Big Zao didn't have the documents she needed to cross the bridge.

In Hekou she met a Vietnamese woman who helped to smuggle her across the river to Lao Cai. It was a few minutes upriver by motorbike, then a quick boat trip across to Vietnam. Nobody asked to see any papers. Big Zao knew she'd paid the woman too much, but she didn't care – she just wanted to go home.

Big Zao arrived back in Sapa, penniless and pregnant, ten months after she'd disappeared.

She spent a week in Sapa and then a year in Hanoi, where she gave birth. Her "husband" had been hoping that their child would be a son – and it was, though he never saw it.

In Hanoi, Big Zao received accommodation, support, and vocational training from Blue Dragon. She didn't know if her kidnapper was ever caught.

Some time later, after Big Zao had returned to live in Sapa, Michael Brosowski had visited the area. He'd wanted to go trekking and had contacted Big Zao, who was working as a guide.

As it happened, Big Zao wasn't available on that particular day. She suggested that Michael go trekking with her niece – and my friend – Vu. As a result, Michael and Vu had spent two days trekking together.

Now, three and a half years after Big Zao had been taken, Vu had also been kidnapped and forced into marriage in China. She knew about her aunt's escape, and knew she'd received support from Blue Dragon.

Vu knew Michael personally, and knew he could help her now – perhaps more than anyone. She knew that Big Zao could put her in touch with him.

All she had to do was find a way to contact Big Zao.

GET FREE

Vu was trapped somewhere in China, with her unemployed "husband" and his video game addiction. She had to find a way to contact her family before she, too, fell pregnant.

In one crucial respect, Vu was lucky: her "husband" had taken no precautions to stop her contacting the outside world. Unlike many trafficked girls, she had access to both a phone and a computer.

Vu remembered Big Zao's phone number, and tried to call her – but she couldn't get through.

It was Vu's first time outside Vietnam, and she didn't know anything about international dialling codes. Vu punched in her aunt's number again and again, but the phone just wouldn't connect, and she was left crying in confusion.

Locking herself in the bedroom where her "husband"

kept a second computer, Vu struggled to make sense of its unfamiliar Chinese programs, where everything was written in an alien script.

It took Vu several months to access her email account and find her list of contacts. She sent a series of messages to her friends in Vietnam and Australia, pleading for help.

Vu cried when she received the first response, from a friend in Hanoi. Vu's friend helped her understand the dialling codes, and gave her the "0084" prefix she'd been missing. Vu took a pen, scribbled the numbers on her hand, ran downstairs, and finally succeeded in calling Big Zao.

Vu described their first conversation: "My aunty say, 'Who are this?'. I say, 'Do you know who are me?'. She say, 'Do you Vu?'. I say, 'Yes.' She say, 'Do you know where do you are? Do you know which country you are?' I say, 'I don't know. I don't know where is here.'"

Vu also rang her mother's home in the village. Her step-father called her mother down from the rice terraces, and mother and daughter cried together on the phone.

Malcolm, an Australian friend living in Hanoi, showed Vu how to check the IP address of her computer. He learned that Vu was somewhere in the general area of Nanjing, 2,400 kilometres by road from Sapa, and passed this information to Blue Dragon.

Vu had been sold to her "husband" under a false name. Vu's "husband" didn't know her real name, and didn't know where she was originally from. He first realised she was from Vietnam when he received a phone bill with hundreds of dollars' worth of calls and text messages to Sapa and Hanoi.

Although Vu could speak little Chinese and struggled to communicate with her "husband" or his family, it was clear they were worried she would try to run away, and began monitoring her emails. Vu did everything she could to assure them she had no intention of leaving.

Meanwhile, of course, she was planning her escape.

Every time that Blue Dragon had rescued a girl from China, it had been the work of a lone operative – always the same man. This man was the very definition of a hero, risking his life on a regular basis to bring kidnapped girls home to their families in Vietnam.

I have the deepest admiration and respect for this man. Because of the nature of his work, I can't tell you his name, so let's call him X.

Over the years, X had singlehandedly rescued dozens of Vietnamese girls from Chinese brothels – but this operation would be a very unusual one.

This time, X would be accompanied by a second operative. They would be rescuing a girl who had been forced not into prostitution, but marriage. In fact, they were hoping to rescue not one but two girls, in two different locations – Vu and May.

The two operatives entered China, and established themselves in a hotel in Nanjing – a vast city of seven million people.

Vu's "husband" and his family were watching Vu closely. The only thing protecting her was the family's assumption that Vu wouldn't be foolish enough to escape, because she had neither the money nor the language skills to make it home. She needed to be very careful not to further arouse their suspicions.

Vu didn't have a phone of her own, and didn't have any phone contacts in China. When she made calls, she used her "husband's" phone, or his mother's. If the family saw Vu was receiving calls from a local number, they would be alerted that something unusual was happening.

As a precaution, the two operatives in Nanjing communicated with her indirectly, relaying their messages via Blue Dragon's headquarters in Vietnam. They spent several days speaking secretly to Vu, trying to narrow down her location.

In the months since her arrival, Vu had been given a little more freedom to leave the house on occasion, and had become familiar with parts of her immediate area. She was somewhere near an airport. If she could note the times of take-offs and landings, Blue Dragon's operatives could check all nearby flight schedules and perhaps identify the airport, and where Vu was in relation to it.

Ideally, they would find a public location where they could arrange a rendezvous, not far from the house where Vu was living. They would go there in a rented car, and the Vietnamese team would notify Vu when they were in position.

Vu would have to find an opportunity to slip away from the house. If she could reach the rendezvous, Blue Dragon's operatives could extract her from the area.

But the operatives didn't have enough clues, and couldn't identify the area where Vu was being kept. They decided not to approach the Chinese police – without any local contacts, they didn't know how the police might react, and didn't think they'd be able to help.

They had a back-up plan, but it carried more risk for Vu. She'd have to steal her "husband's" phone, get out of the house, and make her way to the taxi rank at the local markets. If she was lucky, there would be a taxi already waiting.

Nobody knew how the family would react if they caught Vu lying to them, stealing from them, and trying to run away. She knew it was risky, and she'd have only one chance – but she decided to take it. She sent word to Blue Dragon's operatives that she'd leave as soon as possible.

Pocketing her wedding DVD and her "husband's" phone, Vu told her "husband" she was going out to find his mother, who had left the house a few minutes earlier. She slipped outside – and then she ran.

The family was quickly alerted to her absence. They called the middlemen from whom they'd originally bought Vu, the two Chinese Hmong men she'd found so terrifying. The middlemen called Vu and told her she'd never make it home to Vietnam, that they'd hunt her down and kill her.

Vu kept running.

TAKE THE LONG WAY HOME

Blue Dragon's operatives, waiting anxiously in their hotel room in Nanjing, finally received a call from Vu saying she'd escaped and was safely inside a taxi. They gave instructions to the driver, and – after a journey of more than an hour – the taxi pulled up outside their hotel.

By this time, Blue Dragon's operatives had discovered that the only information they'd received in relation to May had been incorrect, and there was no hope of finding her. In any case, with Vu's traffickers alerted to her escape, they had to get Vu back across the border as soon as possible. She wasn't safe yet.

It was a two-thousand kilometre journey back to the nearest Vietnamese border crossing, and Vu didn't have a Chinese identity card. To avoid any scattered checkpoints, the three of them spent days travelling by bus through the backroads of China.

I later had an opportunity to speak with X about his rescue work. Although the rescues were highly stressful and often quite dramatic, he felt privileged to witness the change that girls experienced during their first moments of freedom.

Most of the girls gave little thought to themselves, he said. As soon as they were in a safe situation, all they wanted to do was to call home and let their parents know they were okay. Some wanted to stop and buy presents for their families. Many opened up to him about the details of their experiences, while others – especially those forced to work late nights in the brothels – just wanted to sleep.

Vu's traffickers had threatened to catch her and kill her, and Blue Dragon was taking that threat seriously. If they could get Vu home, she could help them identify and prosecute her traffickers. The traffickers knew that, and would do whatever they could to stop her getting back to Vietnam. Vu would be most vulnerable when crossing the border.

There were three major border crossings between China and Vietnam. There was a very real risk that Vu's traffickers would be watching the Lao Cai border crossing near Sapa, so that was quickly ruled out as an option.

The two remaining alternatives were both northeast of Hanoi – one on the coast, and one inland. Blue Dragon's operatives had to choose one, without knowing if the traffickers would have agents there waiting for them.

Vu had no papers, no way of proving her identity, and her family had never reported her abduction to the authorities, which further complicated the matter.

Using their contacts, Blue Dragon arranged the necessary paperwork with Vu's family and the Vietnamese government. They coordinated a formal handover ceremony between the authorities on both sides of the border, and the party crossed without incident.

Vu was back on Vietnamese soil.

With the traffickers searching for her, it wasn't safe for Vu to return to Sapa immediately. She spent several weeks living in Hanoi with her friend Malcolm and his partner, while Blue Dragon facilitated sessions with a psychologist, a lawyer, and the police.

Ultimately, Vu's traffickers couldn't be identified: they never caught her, but they were never caught, either.

Vu had spent six months in China, and had been back in Sapa for sixteen months when I spoke to her.

On the surface, she seemed like any other fully-functioning adult – yet it was clear that her experience had affected her in profound and lasting ways. While Vu had physically returned home, her life could never go back to the way it had been. She no longer seemed to know where she fit into her community, or how to move forward with her life.

The world of human trafficking was so much more complex than I'd ever imagined – and the more I saw, the more complex it became. Vu's situation had been simple by comparison to May and Pang's current situations in China.

May and Pang had been gone for years, and it seemed they'd both given birth in China. I could spend all my time and money investigating their abductions, and could risk my life trying to find them – but could I actually do anything to help them?

I didn't know, but there was only one way to find out. All I could do was to keep pushing forward, one step at a time.

ALREADY GONE

As I gradually reached out to more of May's friends, each of them echoed what Chu and Chan had told me. Nobody seemed to know who had kidnapped May, or how.

I decided to risk a meeting with May's boyfriend, Chinh, to hear his version of events. Chan helped to arrange the meeting and came with me to interpret, as Chinh spoke little English.

There was no doubt that the circle of people closest to May – including her friends, and her own family – had been infiltrated by the traffickers. Each time I met with someone from that circle, I didn't know whether I was meeting with a friend and potential ally, or with the insider who had betrayed May to the traffickers. I had to approach with caution and, in the absence of concrete facts, rely on my instincts.

I met with Chinh at a farmhouse on the outskirts of Sapa. He was a well-mannered, softly-spoken young man with a Beatles haircut and the hint of a moustache on his upper lip.

My gut feeling told me that Chinh wasn't involved with the traffickers, and I ruled him out as a suspect in May's disappearance. At the same time, however, I was sure that Chinh wasn't being entirely honest with me. His version of events simply didn't fit with other accounts I'd heard.

Chu and Chan had told me how Chinh had been madly in love with May, and how he'd wept when she'd disappeared.

When Chinh began speaking, however, he seemed oddly indifferent towards May and their relationship. He played down his feelings for May, describing her as "not a bad girl, but not a very good one". He claimed he'd never cried for her, and hadn't been particularly worried when she'd disappeared.

Behind his nonchalance, I sensed that May and her disappearance had impacted Chinh deeply – perhaps more than he was willing to admit even to himself.

Chinh recalled how he'd first seen May in the park in Sapa, in early 2011, and had been attracted to her.

At that time, Chinh was nineteen, and May was about fifteen. While four years is a significant age gap between teenagers, it wasn't unusual for Hmong men to choose younger partners. This seemed to be the rule, rather than the exception.

A friend had given Chinh May's number, he'd called her, and they'd soon begun dating. He'd been May's boyfriend for about five months, until her disappearance.

In Sapa, the terms "boyfriend" and "girlfriend" could mean many different things.

There were many young Hmong people living in Sapa, away from parental supervision. Pre-marital sex, while traditionally forbidden, certainly existed.

Yet the majority of young couples still seemed to have very conservative attitudes, and wouldn't even kiss or hold hands before marriage. When Chinh described his relationship with May, it struck me as very innocent – almost like a primary school romance.

It was only natural for a young woman May's age to take an interest in boys – but it was also necessary to keep a boyfriend hidden from her family. If May's parents had learned about Chinh, May would have been judged and shamed, and pressured to leave him.

As I later learned, May's parents were completely unaware she'd had a boyfriend, seemed scandalised by the idea, and flatly refused to believe it.

By contrast, there was no shame in a young man having a girlfriend. May had been to Chinh's village and met his parents several times.

Chinh confessed that he'd loved May and planned to marry her – despite the fact that his family were Catholics, while May's family still followed traditional shamanism.

It seemed that Chinh's feelings had been stronger

than May's, who wasn't sure whether she'd loved him or not.

Chinh struck me as a serious young man who might offer a stable but unexciting relationship. I could understand why a restless fifteen-year-old might have had her doubts and hesitations in committing to a long-term relationship with him.

May's indecision seemed to be a constant source of tension between them, and their relationship had been plagued by drama. Chinh had been jealous of how friendly May had been with other young men, and complained that she was constantly speaking to them on the phone.

He recalled a time he'd gone to visit May at the room she rented, only to find her there with another young man. When Chinh had stormed out, May had chased him, insisting the other man was only a friend. Chinh was certain she'd been lying to him, and had been seeing someone else behind his back.

But that wasn't his only concern. At that time, more and more girls were disappearing from Sapa, and Chinh was afraid May might also be taken.

I could only imagine what a strange situation that must have been. A relationship could be complex enough without the constant fear that your partner could be kidnapped at any time.

Sadly, Chinh's fear was justified, and his relationship with May had ended very abruptly one evening.

Chinh had been attending evening Mass at the

church on Sapa's main square. May tried twice to call him there, but he hadn't been able to answer.

After the service finished at half past seven, Chinh was scheduled to work the night shift behind the reception desk at a nearby hotel. As he walked down Cau May Street towards the hotel, he tried twice to call May back. Her phone rang but she didn't answer. The third time Chinh tried to call, May's phone was unavailable – switched off, or out of range.

At that moment, he was approached by one of May's friends, a girl named Xa. Xa asked if Chinh had seen May, and he said no.

Xa told him what she knew. That morning, another young Hmong man had invited May to go with him to the Silver Waterfall, and May had accepted. Xa had been with May at the time. She'd met the man, and spoken to him.

When night had fallen and May was nowhere to be found, Xa suspected that the man had kidnapped May to sell her in China.

Chinh wanted to start searching for May immediately, but he had to start work. From the hotel, he began calling May's friends, asking if they'd seen her. Nobody had. Chu said she was first alerted to May's disappearance when Chinh called her in tears, desperate for any news.

The next day, there was still no sign of May. Chinh had gone around Sapa in search of more information, but hadn't learned anything. As the days became weeks, it seemed certain that May had been sold in China.

In the wake of her disappearance – as so often happened – people began spreading vicious rumours about May, blaming her disappearance on her own indecent behaviour.

Chinh said he hadn't felt anything during that time, which I found difficult to believe.

He'd heard that kidnapped girls were forced to marry old men, or to work hard in some terrible job, and he'd felt a little sorry about that. He wouldn't have wanted anything like that to happen to May – but he said that May had lied to him and treated him badly, so he put all thought of her behind him and moved on with his life.

Six months later, Chinh had begun dating another young Hmong woman, who converted to Catholicism for him. They'd married thirteen months after May's disappearance, and were now raising their first child.

After learning that Chinh had married, I could understand why he'd been so reticent about his feelings for May. Whatever he felt for her was a secret known only to himself, and it seemed best that way.

I thanked Chinh for sharing his story, and went in search of May's friend Xa.

STEALING MY HEART

Xa wasn't one of the ten girls from May's group.

While she and I had met in passing, we'd never spoken about May's disappearance. It now seemed that Xa was the last person to have seen May in Sapa, and had even met May's kidnapper.

Could she give me the clues I needed to identify the kidnapper, and to identify the insider who had betrayed May and her friends to the traffickers?

I found Xa in her rented room. It was a small, dimly-lit room with a series of old photographs taped to one bare concrete wall. I saw pictures of May and Pang, smiling by the lake in Sapa.

While she didn't want to be filmed, Xa agreed to speak with me, and consented to an audio recording of the conversation.

Xa presented herself well, in a very clean, new Black

Hmong outfit. Beneath her fashionable haircut, her scrubbed skin, and her silver jewellery, I saw the girl who had grown hard and strong amongst the rice terraces, and the young woman who had watched her friends disappear from Sapa.

May and Xa's families were related by marriage, and the two had known each other since they were little girls. In the months before May's abduction, Xa had been spending a lot of time with May, and had seen May's kidnapper on several occasions.

I learned that May had been meeting with her kidnapper for two or three weeks before he'd taken her. She'd had a crush on him and wanted to be with him, though she was already in a relationship with Chinh.

With the possible exception of Zao, it seemed that none of May's other friends had met her kidnapper, because May herself had been hiding him.

I was surprised to learn that May had been in relationships – however innocent they may have been – with not one, but two young men. I'd never pictured her as a very secretive person. I supposed if you looked at anyone's life closely enough, you were likely to find a few unexpected things.

To the local Hmong community – and particularly the elder generation – I realised that the very fact of these relationships would be considered damning evidence against May. She would be judged for having spent time alone with young men, and blamed for her own kidnapping.

It was grossly unfair to hold May responsible for the things that had happened to her. It was true that she had taken risks, and I could understand why Chinh had been upset with her – but May was a girl fumbling her way through the world of teenage romance, and every relationship was a risk in Sapa. I certainly hadn't understood much about relationships when I was fifteen.

I couldn't help but wonder how different May's life might have been if she'd chosen Chinh over the trafficker. What huge and permanent changes had hinged upon the flutterings of a teenage girl's heart.

Xa tried to remember what the kidnapper had called himself – she thought it was Veng. She guessed he'd been in his early twenties, perhaps six or seven years older than May.

He was a thin man, with a long, distinctive face. He'd worn Western-style clothing, and had claimed to be from Lao Cai.

Xa had been suspicious of Veng. She'd asked May whether she was afraid that Veng might take her to China – but May was convinced he was a good man, and hadn't seemed worried at all.

It seemed that Chinh had learned about Veng just two days before May's disappearance, and had been upset with May. Was this when Chinh had discovered May with another man in her room? I wasn't sure.

On the day before May's disappearance, she'd planned to go to Hanoi with Chan, so they could study together. Chan had told me that May had changed her mind at the last moment, and had stayed in Sapa to be with her boyfriend.

At that time, neither Chan nor I had known that May had been seeing someone else. Now, I realised it was Veng, not Chinh, that May had stayed to be with.

On the day she disappeared, Xa met May's kidnapper – it was the first and only time they'd actually spoken together. Veng had invited them both to come with him to the Silver Waterfall. Xa didn't trust him, and didn't want to go, so May had gone alone.

That was around 9am. It seemed that the waterfall trip was a way for May's kidnapper to build trust with her – and it worked, just as it had worked with Chan's sister and cousin.

The Silver Waterfall was just twelve kilometres from Sapa, in the opposite direction to the border crossing at Lao Cai. It was a popular tourist attraction visible from the main road, which made it a safe, cheap, and easy trip from Sapa. A Hmong girl was unlikely to feel threatened or uncomfortable there.

Offering to take a girl to the Silver Waterfall was a common way for a young Hmong man to indicate his romantic interest, and the motorbike trip there and back would give him plenty of time to speak to her. For a trafficker, it was an ideal opportunity to win a little more trust from his target, in preparation for the kidnapping itself.

After visiting the waterfall, Veng had brought May back to Sapa. Xa saw her again – for the last time – at around 11am in Sapa's main square. A boy from their village had also seen May in the square, at around 3pm that afternoon.

It seemed that May and Veng had spent the afternoon together in Sapa, and she'd gone with him on his bike again that evening – only this time, they hadn't come back.

Xa never saw May or Veng again. She said Veng had a very distinctive face, but couldn't describe him very well for me, and didn't know how we could possibly identify him.

If I'd returned to Sapa sooner, Xa might have helped me construct a composite sketch of Veng's face. With a clear image of what the man looked like, we could have enlisted the help of the authorities, to begin a search for him throughout the borderlands.

Could we have found Veng, and learned where he'd sold May?

We'll never know. Too much time had passed, Xa's memories had faded, and that line of investigation was now closed.

There was another hope – that Xa could help me identify the insider who had introduced May to her kidnapper. But Xa said she didn't know how May and Veng had first met, and I hit another dead end.

My investigation seemed hopeless, but I realised there was still one final possibility.

Xa, and the boy from her village, had been the last people to see May – but they hadn't been the last to speak to her.

Chinh hadn't been able to call May on the night she disappeared – but Zao had.

If anyone could tell me more, it would be Zao.

AN HONEST MISTAKE

Zao was the person I'd most wanted to meet with in Sapa. After May's abduction, Zao had become my closest contact within their group.

Zao was May's cousin, and had been closest to May and Pang before they'd been kidnapped. She was the one who had first told me of May's abduction, and – according to everyone I'd spoken to – she knew the most about it.

She also seemed to know the most about May's phonecall from China, and had recently given me both May and Pang's Chinese phone numbers.

Chu and Chan had passed me Zao's phone number, and we'd been in contact – but, for whatever reason, it had been difficult to arrange a meeting with her.

I'd been deeply impressed, and greatly encouraged, by Chu and Chan's understanding and passion for the cause. Perhaps I'd been overly suspicious of the girls. Zao was an intelligent young woman who'd lost five close friends to human trafficking. I was certain I could confide in her, and count on her for support.

In fact, there was a good chance that Zao had already guessed what I was doing in Sapa, and why. It made little sense to hide my true purpose from her. Zao could be a valuable ally – she could help me, perhaps, more than anyone.

At last, Zao agreed to meet me outside Sapa's market.

In the three and a half years since I'd last seen her, Zao had grown taller, and had traded her traditional Hmong clothing for a black jacket and blue denim jeans. Her cheeks were pockmarked with acne scars, and there was a guarded distance in her eyes.

Zao didn't come alone to our rendezvous – with her was a sullen young Hmong man. Though Zao didn't introduce him, it was clear that he was her boyfriend.

This was something new to me – so far as I knew, none of my Hmong friends had had boyfriends when I'd last been living in Sapa, and I'd never seen them walking in the streets with any of the local boys. I was surprised that Zao and her boyfriend went about so openly in the centre of Sapa, with premarital relations so heavily frowned upon by the local community.

Having spent their childhoods conversing with tourists and competing with each other for sales, my Hmong friends were quick and lively. They spoke smatterings of several languages, and had an understanding of the world beyond Sapa. Zao, in particular, had always struck me as a particularly intelligent girl.

The lives of the local Hmong men, however, were dominated by the alternating seasons of manual labour and lethargy in the villages. They generally seemed to have little understanding of, or interest in, the outside world.

Zao's boyfriend looked like an uncultivated sort of village boy, and I found it a little unsettling to see them together. It seemed tragic that such bright and promising young women would spend their lives in submission to such men – but what alternatives did they have?

Occasionally, one of the Hmong women might have the opportunity to marry a foreigner, and would almost always do so. The rest of the young women had little option but to marry local men, and return to the villages.

I asked Zao if I could speak to her alone, somewhere private. She said it was okay to speak in front of her boyfriend, as he spoke no English. I believed her – it was uncommon for the local Hmong men to speak more than a few words of English, and her boyfriend didn't seem particularly educated.

A friend's family owned a hotel nearby. I'd arranged to use one of the rooms, and felt that would be the best place to speak.

I asked Zao and her boyfriend to step in off the street, but something had put Zao on guard, and she stopped short of the entrance. She didn't seem to like my secretive behaviour – and neither did I. I made a snap decision to tell her everything right then and there, on the street outside the hotel.

Quickly, simply, and in a low voice, I told Zao why I'd come back to Sapa, and what I was trying to do there. I wanted to find out what had happened to May and Pang, and wanted to do everything I could to help them. I knew that she had information that could help me, and that's why I wanted to speak to her.

Zao's boyfriend grunted something in Hmong. She turned to him, and they spoke briefly in their own language.

Turning back to me, Zao made it clear she wasn't interested in helping me, and wasn't going to tell me anything. With no further explanation, she turned on her heel and walked away, her boyfriend close behind. Left standing in shock and incomprehension, I watched them disappear around the corner.

Afterwards, I called Zao to try to understand what had happened. She flatly refused to speak to me.

Was Zao working with the kidnappers? I didn't want to believe it – but she certainly wasn't working with me against them, as you might expect of someone who'd had so many close friends taken.

I tried to reason it out. To my mind, Zao's behaviour didn't necessarily mean she was in league with the traffickers – but it did mean the traffickers were very close, and now I'd blown my cover.

Zao knew something, that much was clear to me. Perhaps she knew too much about May and Pang's kidnappers, and was afraid of what they might do to her if they caught her sharing information with me.

I wondered, too, about her boyfriend. Who was he, and what part did he play in all this? I didn't know.

Gradually, I reached out to more of my Hmong friends. I dropped May's name, and the facts of her abduction, into seemingly-casual conversations, and worked slowly and patiently towards the information I sought. I danced around the subject, letting the girls tell the stories of their own volition.

All enquiries led back to the same point: Zao. All of the girls told me that Zao had been closest to May, was the last person she'd spoken to, and had the best information about her abduction.

As May's other friends gradually became aware of my true purpose in Sapa, they all supported my cause. They wanted May back as much as I did, and they wanted to give me the best chance of helping her. From time to time, one of them would reach out to Zao and plead with her to speak to me, or try to pry the information out of her themselves.

As some of the girls succeeded in gleaning pieces of information from Zao, her story began breaking apart. Zao denied knowledge of any contact from May, and denied having her phone number. Some of the things she'd told me before my arrival in Sapa proved to be untrue. It remained a mystery how and when Zao had obtained May's number, or any news of her.

At first I made excuses for Zao, then I became very

uncertain of her behaviour. I'd heard plenty of conflicting rumours in Sapa, but Zao's story just didn't add up. One friend, who had been with Zao very soon after May's disappearance, recalled that Zao had seemed especially cold, detached, and uncaring at the time – especially for someone who had supposedly been May's best friend.

As the weeks passed, Zao's silence deepened. Not only did she refuse to speak to me, she refused to speak about me to anyone else, and refused to speak about what had happened to May. If anyone – even her closest friends – raised the subject, Zao would simply hang up, or walk away.

None of us could understand it, but we could all agree on one thing: Zao's behaviour was extremely strange, and more than a little suspicious. So long as Zao refused to speak to me, there seemed to be no hope of identifying May's trafficker, and there didn't seem to be any other way of finding May.

What was Zao hiding? What did she know that she refused to tell us?

IT'S A MAN'S MAN'S MAN'S WORLD

Young Hmong women were not the only ones at risk of being trafficked from Sapa, but there was one custom that left them especially vulnerable: the custom of *zij poj niam*.

While often referred to in English as "bride kidnapping", that term was misleading. The victim did not become a bride until long after her kidnapping, if at all. "Marriage by abduction" was a more accurate description.

Kidnapping was part of Hmong culture. If an unmarried man saw a girl he liked, he could gather his friends to help snatch her from the street. He'd then take her back to his family home and keep her there.

Any girl of marriageable age could be taken – and, in Hmong communities, a girl could be married as young as twelve or thirteen. The only thing a man had to know about his victim was that she wasn't already married.

It could be days before the girl's family found out where she was. The man's family would send word to the girl's father, telling him his daughter had been kidnapped, and asking what price he wanted for her.

Like footbinding in China or bullfighting in Spain, the tradition of marriage by abduction was a destructive one. It caused harm not only to those directly involved, but to Hmong society as a whole.

Legally speaking – because of the girl's age, her unwillingness to marry, and the lack of any paperwork – many of the marriages in Sapa were no more legitimate than the "marriages" that kidnapped girls were forced into in China. In Sapa, however, the lines were often blurred, and it was far more difficult to make a clear distinction.

Sometimes the girl knew her abductor, had a relationship with him, and was willing to marry him. Even so, for the sake of her honour as a respectable young woman, she would be compelled to struggle during the kidnapping.

This could make it very difficult for an onlooker to understand if a victim's struggles were genuine or just a pretence.

Even if the girl was willing to marry her kidnapper, the abduction itself was an act of shocking force which was degrading and often painful for the girl. Her fear might have been very real, even if her struggle was not.

The days that followed the abduction were often a

terrifying time for the girl, as she was held captive in the man's home. She was supposedly under the protection of one of his female relatives – his mother, perhaps, or a sister – but sometimes things went tragically wrong, resulting in the girl's rape or suicide.

In theory, the girl would have a choice whether to marry her kidnapper or not. In reality, however, she would often be heavily pressured by one or both families, or her own desires might simply be ignored.

The custom of marriage by abduction was a violation of a girl's most basic human rights, and could be considered a form of human trafficking in itself. Worse still, in many regions – including Sapa – it also facilitated the cross-border trafficking of vulnerable young women.

If a girl disappeared, and was being trafficked for sale as a bride or prostitute in China, her parents would often believe she'd been abducted for marriage within her own community.

During those crucial first hours, rather than enlist the help of the authorities to begin the search for their daughter, they would simply stay at home and wait for news of her.

Several days could pass before the girl's parents realised their mistake, and by that time it was already far too late – they had no way of finding their daughter, and might never see her again. Once a girl had been taken across the border, there was very little that anyone in Vietnam could do.

A family's only real hope of catching their daughter's

traffickers was to approach the authorities as soon as they learned of her disappearance. A description of the girl could then be passed along the border, alerting the police and border guards to the suspected abduction.

But the custom of marriage by abduction muddied the waters. Even if the girl's family did approach the authorities immediately after their daughter disappeared, the police wouldn't know if she was being held in one of the local villages for marriage, or being trafficked across the border for sale in China. They wouldn't know how best to respond – and, with a chance that the kidnapping was cultural, they often wouldn't want to get involved.

There were cases of family members who had acted quickly to help their kidnapped daughter – only to be dismissed by the authorities, who told them to come back in three or four days. By that time, the situation would be clearer, but the narrow window of opportunity to help the girl would have long since closed.

At the time of my investigation, about three-quarters of all Hmong marriages in Sapa were the result of an abduction, perhaps more. Chu estimated that for every girl that went willingly with her abductor, two others were taken against their will.

If a young couple was already in a relationship, the young man could approach the girl's father for permission to marry his daughter. Those who took advantage of the custom of marriage by abduction were often the less desirable men, who otherwise had more limited options for finding a bride.

It was easy to see the trap that held young Hmong women. By the time a girl became a teenager, she was considered marriageable, and could be kidnapped by any unmarried man, at any time. Naturally, she would prefer to spend her life with a man she knew and cared about, rather than a stranger. She struggled to find a young man who might love her before anyone abducted her – yet her culture forbade her from having a boyfriend, and gave her few opportunities to interact with young men. The girl didn't know who to trust, her community would shame her for having a partner, and a hidden relationship was even more dangerous for her. If her "boyfriend" kidnapped her and sold her across the border, the girl would be blamed for ever having spoken to him. She was surrounded by danger and double standards on all sides, and the weight of the community was against her.

To evolve and flourish in an ever-changing world – as individuals, as societies, and as a species – we need to continually question our habits and customs, and discard those which have become harmful to us.

Interestingly, I was told that marriage by abduction was not the long-held tradition some claimed it to be – in fact, it appeared to be a relatively new convention.

It seemed that Hmong marriages had previously been arranged by the fathers of the bride and groom. I was told that rebellious young men had begun challenging their fathers' authority by seizing girls of their own choosing, and bringing them back to their family homes. As the girl had already been taken, it was too late for the father to intervene, and he would have to respect his son's wishes. In time, this had become an accepted practice.

If such a violent custom could so easily be added to a culture, then it could also be removed.

Change was nothing new for the Hmong people. They'd left China, the lowlands, their opium crops, and their semi-nomadic lifestyles behind. These changes had largely been forced upon them – but if they were capable of making such dramatic changes for the sake of others, surely they were capable of changing for their own benefit.

And, in fact, they were. In Laos, I'd visited Hmong villages where the custom of marriage by abduction had been recognised as a destructive one, and had been successfully stopped by the village elders.

Even in Sapa, the Hmong families that had converted to Christianity had stopped the practice amongst themselves. The rest of the Hmong community there, however, had not even begun to address the issue, and seemed to consider it beyond question.

For their daughters, being grabbed and hauled away by a stranger was a very real fear which could become reality at any time.

NEW YEAR'S DAY

The biggest annual celebration in Sapa was the Lunar New Year.

The Kinh called it Tet. It was a week-long celebration which would arrive with the new moon towards the end of winter, at the same time as the Chinese New Year.

This was a very special time for the Hmong communities. All of the villagers had new outfits, which had taken months to create and were now being worn for the first time. The freshly-dyed indigo was so dark it seemed almost black, the embroidered reds, greens, and whites were at their most vivid, and the outer jackets had been polished across broad stones to a bright sheen.

One peculiarity of the New Year celebrations was that young men and women could socialise freely without being judged by their elders.

Until recent years, the local Hmong people had

walked each week from their villages to the Sunday market in Sapa, and afterwards they had walked home again. Along the way, young men and women had found opportunities to speak together, and to meet potential partners.

These days, however, almost everyone would come to Sapa by motorbike, and those opportunities no longer existed. Now, the New Year's celebrations were a young woman's best chance to meet a boyfriend – but it could also be a very dangerous time for her.

The New Year was an ideal time for a young Hmong man to kidnap a bride.

Every day for a week, at least two or three girls would be abducted from Sapa and its surrounding villages. Sometimes four or five girls were taken in a single day.

On the final day of the festival, there were celebrations in the villages with singing, dancing, and games. This was considered a "dragon day" – a particularly auspicious day to kidnap a bride – and more abductions happened on this day than any other.

Unless a man had a particular target in mind, he might simply mingle with the crowd, looking for a girl he found attractive.

There was very little a girl could do to protect herself from a kidnapper. Chu and Chan told me their best strategy was to be rude to any man that approached them. A man would be less likely to snatch a woman who refused to speak to him, they reasoned – yet admitted what poor protection it really was. They could still very easily fall prey to any man who wanted to take them.

It was horrifying that these intelligent, educated young women might be violently carried away at any time by even the most ignorant farm boy, simply because he liked the shape of them.

If he caught his victim alone, a man would need only three or four friends to kidnap her – one to grab each of the girl's hands, and the others to shove away anyone who might try to help her.

If the girl was with friends, however, a man would need a larger group to physically overpower them. In some cases, it became a savage tug-of-war between the two groups, with ten or twenty people on either side.

Sometimes the kidnappers carried money, and would try to bribe anyone who wanted to help the girl. At other times, it was shockingly violent, with the two groups furiously hitting, kicking, and biting one another, fighting for possession of the girl.

I was told that a girl's friends could often be bribed, while her family was more likely to fight.

Once the girl had been seized, she might be loaded onto the back of a motorbike, or the kidnapper might take her back to his village on foot, shoving her along in a forced march. Sometimes one of the bigger men would simply heft her up on his shoulders and run with her, as if she were a sack of rice.

Chan described the abduction of a "very, very poor girl" she'd witnessed in her own village. The girl had been alone when perhaps fifteen young men had suddenly converged on her. She'd tried to flee in terror, and they'd stormed after her. After realising she couldn't escape, the girl had thrown herself on the ground and tried to dig her fingers into the earth, scratching around desperately for something to hold onto. As the men pulled at her, the girl's clothes had been torn open, and still nobody came to help her. The men had dragged her away, still crying and screaming.

The Vietnamese Hmong tend not to be very expressive of their emotions, but Chan said she herself had very nearly been brought to tears by the girl's terror and helplessness in the face of her attackers.

In 2014, the New Year fell at the end of January – two weeks after my arrival in Sapa – with celebrations spilling over into the first week of February.

Vu was terrified that she'd be abducted during the festival. The previous year, a man had told her if he saw her on the streets, he would kidnap her. She'd been so scared she'd spent almost all of her time with trekking groups, taking only three days off in the entire month.

If she was with a group of foreigners, she'd reasoned, the man wouldn't have the audacity to try to kidnap her. But she'd been wrong – the man had grabbed her one day in the village, and Vu had only managed to escape him thanks to the timely intervention of her trekking group.

Another friend, who prefers to remain anonymous, had been targeted by a man she barely knew and didn't like at all. On the morning of the "dragon day", she'd heard a rumour that the man was planning to kidnap her. In fear, she'd avoided the festival entirely.

It seems the man had been more interested in taking advantage of the lucky day than in taking any particular girl. When he hadn't been able to find my friend at the festival, he'd simply switched targets, and had kidnapped her cousin instead. They were now married.

One year, Chan and her friend had both been scared of being abducted. Chan had avoided the "dragon day" altogether, spending the day trekking with a tourist. Chan's friend had gone to the festival, and had tried another tactic to protect herself. She'd borrowed a friend's baby and carried it on her back, certain that no one would molest her if she was carrying a baby.

A man she knew but didn't like had followed her all day at the festival. Everywhere she went, she saw his friends and relatives watching her, but they didn't dare touch her so long as she had the baby.

Later that evening, they'd finally caught her alone, and she'd been dragged off to the man's house.

For three days, she'd wept and refused to eat. She'd been given permission to call Chan and, under the watchful eye of a chaperone, was permitted to meet her for an hour by the lake in Sapa. The girl had cried the whole time, saying she didn't want to marry, and would rather die.

Ultimately, however, she had married the man who'd kidnapped her. There was a rumour that his family had used magic to make her fall in love with him. It's more likely, however, that the girl had succumbed to pressure from her own family, and realised she'd had no better alternatives.

If a girl had been abducted but not married, her reputation was tarnished. Having slept in the home of another man – even against her will – she would be perceived as damaged goods.

Once she'd been abducted, a girl's own family would often pressure her into marriage, even if the man was a complete stranger. They feared that if she didn't marry her kidnapper, she'd have few other options for marriage. The only men who might still want to marry her would be those who were less desirable themselves – divorcés and widowers who already had children by a previous marriage, for example.

Often a girl's family seemed less interested in their daughter's wishes than in the bride price they would receive for her. Sometimes a family didn't seem to care what their daughter felt, and she wasn't given a choice at all: it was the father who decided, not the girl.

For some girls, the only hope of escape was to take the "poison leaf", a local plant commonly used to commit suicide.

UNDER PRESSURE

When the New Year arrived, some of my Kinh friends invited Marinho and me to join their celebrations.

We spent a night in Toan's family home, and another with Huong's family in their village on the flatlands. We spent an afternoon with my godson and his parents, who had returned to Sapa for the holidays.

The rest of the week we spent amongst the Hmong people – by the lake, in the square, at the market, and in the villages. The streets were all teeming with young Hmong women and men in their brand new outfits, and we recorded hours of beautiful footage.

As horrific as it sounds, however, what Marinho and I were really hoping to see was a kidnapping.

The custom of marriage by abduction was an important part of the story we wanted to tell in our documentary. It wouldn't be enough to merely explain the practice to an audience: the only way to convey its true horror was to capture it on camera.

The weather was beautiful, and it felt terribly morbid to be walking among the festive locals in their shiny new clothes, watching for signs of potential violence. Marinho and I each worked alone, to increase our chances of witnessing an abduction.

Dozens of young men were roaming the streets in packs. They would isolate a girl, cutting her off from her friends, or they'd encircle their prey and move in from several directions at once. Sometimes they'd hound a girl over a period of hours or days.

Marinho and I recorded footage of young women being harassed, intimidated, grabbed, and chased, but we couldn't seem to capture an actual kidnapping.

Each day we would return to the hotel empty-handed, and hear rumours of abductions that had happened elsewhere. We never seemed to be in the right place at the right time – yet we persisted, day after day.

One afternoon I was by the lake with a European friend. We were watching a young Hmong man speaking intently with two younger-looking girls on the footpath. It was hard to tell if the girls already knew the man. The taller of the two girls smiled, but it was an awkward, apprehensive smile – the smile of a woman who is trapped in an uncomfortable situation.

Each time the girls tried to break away, the man would move around to put himself directly in their path, holding his arms out to block their escape. He seemed confident and practised, while the girls were kept constantly on the back foot.

We didn't know what was being said between them, but it was clear that the girls wanted to walk one way and the man was trying to shepherd them in the opposite direction. He focused his attention on the taller girl, holding and then pulling at her wrist.

The girls turned away and managed to slip across the road. The man began following them, walking almost on their heels before manoeuvring alongside them. When the girls tried to angle away from him, they found themselves hemmed in by a wall.

Gradually, the gestures became more forceful: the man would grab at the taller girl's arm, and she'd tear it away. He took her hand and held it, while she tried to twist out of his grasp. He clamped his hand on her shoulder possessively.

Focused on evading the man, the girls didn't seem to realise how isolated they'd become from the other young people by the lake. My friend and I followed at a distance, until at last the man cornered his prey against the side of a building.

The taller girl moved to escape, first one way and then the other. The man shifted his weight quickly between his feet, swinging his arms in a way that seemed casual but made it clear that he controlled the situation.

It became a strange dance: the girls would try to dart away, and the man would cut them off. He was still talking to the girls, but not with the same intensity as before. Now that he'd physically dominated his prey, it seemed as though he was merely stalling, waiting for the rest of the pack to arrive.

It was a horrible situation, and seemed certain to end with the abduction of the taller girl. I felt very uncomfortable, merely watching and recording the situation as it unfolded. Until that moment, my interests as a filmmaker and as a human being had dovetailed neatly, but now they came into direct opposition. Was I doing the right thing? I didn't know.

These abductions were happening constantly, and the vast majority of people around the world were blissfully unaware.

If I intervened, I could help that particular girl, but I'd miss my chance to draw attention to the broader issue. On the other hand, if I allowed the girl to be kidnapped, the footage of her abduction could potentially help protect many more girls in the future. By showing people what was happening here, I was sure I could help change it.

I remembered what I'd learned when I'd been picking up garbage. The greatest impact came not from my own efforts, but from the change they inspired in others. In this case, however, I had to choose between acting and inspiring others to act: there was no way to do both.

In the long term, I believed that the greatest impact I could make was by allowing the girl to be taken, and filming her abduction. Possessing that knowledge and acting upon it, however, were two very different things.

Was I really capable of just standing by and watching a girl being violently snatched from the street, just a few steps from where I was standing?

As a filmmaker, I hoped so. As a human being, I hoped not.

Then something unexpected happened.

I'd taken it for granted that the girl would be kidnapped – and so, it seemed, had her would-be kidnapper. He'd become complacent, and careless.

The shorter girl moved to the right and, as the man moved to block her, the taller girl bolted suddenly to the left. In a heartbeat, the man saw his prize slip through his fingers. With no real interest in the shorter girl, he made no move to stop her as she dashed across the road to join her friend.

Together, the two girls hurried back towards the lake – but they didn't get far. As the first man followed behind them, the girls were stopped by a group of young Hmong men coming the other way. Were these the friends the man had been waiting for, to help him kidnap the girl? It wasn't clear.

It was very clear, however, that the taller girl was terrified. She'd leapt out of the frying pan and straight into the fire. Her shorter friend slipped away – perhaps to get help, or perhaps just knowing there was little she could do against so many men. We didn't see her again.

I couldn't watch anymore – I felt compelled to act. Though I knew it was a short-sighted decision, I couldn't just stand by and watch this teenage girl being molested by a group of men. I refused to have that on my conscience.

My friend and I stepped in. Pushing our way towards the girl, we asked if she wanted our help. She said she did. My friend and I stood on either side of her, and the three of us walked away together. The men followed us for a short distance, then gave up, clearly frustrated by our unexpected intervention.

The girl seemed suspicious of me – I didn't know if it was because of the camera equipment I was carrying, or simply the fact that I was male. She seemed more comfortable with my female friend, so I fell back and let them walk ahead.

My friend escorted the girl back to the lake, and she relaxed visibly when she was surrounded by other girls again. There was still no guarantee of safety for her there, but she told us she was fine, and we left her.

I'd forfeited the chance to capture the moment on camera, but knew it would have been impossible for me to act in any other way. If I regretted anything about the episode, it was only that we hadn't intervened sooner.

My friend and I walked down to meet Toan at the Yellow Dragon. Marinho rushed in a short time later, buzzing with excitement. He'd just witnessed an abduction for marriage at close quarters – and had captured the whole thing on camera.

SHE BELONGS TO ME

Marinho had a different attitude towards the abductions, seeming to believe that nobody was in a position to judge another culture. Trying to protect the Hmong girls would mean interfering in their culture – and that was something that we, as outsiders, had no right to do.

I didn't agree. I believe a culture is the sum of individual behaviours, and there are certain behaviours that are universally wrong. This was the concept underlying the Universal Declaration of Human Rights, which affirmed the right to "liberty and the security of person" for all.

No law-abiding citizen should live in fear of being seized and carried away by other people. If altering that particular aspect of the Hmong culture was necessary for the protection of those girls, then I believed that's what should be done.

But Vietnam was not among the group of nations that had written the Universal Declaration of Human Rights, and the Hmong people had played no part in its creation.

While the Declaration was one of the world's most important and widely celebrated documents, it could still be considered an imposition of foreign values on the Hmong people.

Which of us was right, and which of us was wrong?

Like so many things in life, it was a question with no definitive answer – just differing points of view.

Marinho loathed human trafficking just as much as I did. I was surprised that we didn't agree on this point, but in a way I was also glad: it meant that he'd been able to film an abduction, while I'd failed.

Marinho handed me the memory card from his camera. As I loaded it into my laptop, he directed my attention to the most recent video file.

The video began slowly – and then a lot of things happened very quickly. I had to watch the footage several times to catch the details, and to understand what I was seeing.

It showed a girl, perhaps fifteen years old, wearing a traditional Black Hmong costume with cheap plastic slippers. She was standing in full daylight, beside one of the principal streets in the centre of Sapa.

The girl looked like she'd just come from the market – she was carrying a slice of watermelon and a pair of shoes in plastic shopping bags. She was trying to walk away from the town centre, presumably trying to go home.

A young man had blocked her way, refusing to let her pass. He looked several years older, perhaps nineteen. He was wearing a Hmong jacket over a Western-style shirt and pants, with a pair of white sneakers. Though there were perhaps only a few years separating them, the contrast between the two was stark: he was a grown man, while she was still a child.

Several times the girl tried to pass the man, or to cross the road, and he pushed her back. Oddly, though, she didn't go back the way she'd come. She seemed to know the man, but didn't seem quite sure what to do.

The man was clearly waiting for something. He checked his phone, and called out to someone he knew across the street.

A motorbike, driven by another young man, came gliding in and stopped beside them. This was what the man had been waiting for. He grabbed the girl by the front of her jacket – but she twisted out of his grasp, and retreated from the motorbike.

The man took her by the wrist and started dragging her forward. She resisted, stumbling – and almost falling – as she tried to pull away. She was nearly on the ground, making herself as heavy and difficult to move as possible.

A third and fourth young man came rushing in on foot, one from either side. A second motorbike pulled up beside them, with two more young men. There were now six men in total.

Two of the men stayed on the motorbikes, watching the girl struggle fiercely against the other four. She cried aloud as they grabbed her roughly by the arms and an ankle, and tried to wrestle her onto the back of a motorbike. One man grabbed her buttock. When the girl's face could be seen through the tangle of limbs, she looked to be in pain.

After several violent attempts, the four men succeeded in shoving their victim into a sidesaddle position on the back of the first motorbike. Her shopping bags, and one of her shoes, were scattered on the ground.

A seventh man appeared, drawing attention to two other teenage girls who were trying to reach their friend.

What happened next looked odd – the two girls seemed to suddenly turn around and scurry back the way they'd come. Closer examination of the footage showed that one of the men had crouched down and grabbed both girls, with his head between their stomachs and his arms around their hips, and had driven them forcibly away.

Moments later, the two girls hurled themselves back again – first one, and then the other – in a desperate attempt to reach their friend. They were repelled by a wall of young men, who shoved them back.

Meanwhile, the first man and one of his friends had forced their victim to straddle the motorbike. She continued to struggle violently, using the driver as leverage to throw her weight backwards, but it was too late. One of her friends made a final, failed attempt to reach her.

The first man climbed onto the motorbike behind the girl, boxing her in with his arms, and urged the driver to leave. The motorbike pulled away, followed closely by two young men on the second motorbike.

The entire struggle – from the moment the man had first grabbed his victim's jacket, to the moment she was carried away on the motorbike – had taken only sixty seconds.

What shocked me most was not the speed and violence of the abduction. Nor was it the broad grins and laughter of her kidnappers, who very visibly enjoyed manhandling the tiny, defenceless girl. What shocked me most was how commonplace it all seemed.

In the space of those sixty seconds, eleven motorbikes, one car, and several pedestrians had passed by. The only ones who seemed to have taken any notice were two young men who'd stopped to enjoy the spectacle. One had stood chewing sugarcane within easy reach of the girl, in the same way that you or I might munch popcorn while watching TV.

As I rewatched the video over the following hours and days, I couldn't help but wonder where the girl was at that moment, and what she might be going through. Had she agreed to marry the man? How was she being treated by his family? Was she physically safe?

Having now seen the footage countless times, I still

can't say how the girl felt about her kidnapper. I have no doubt that her fear and pain were real, and her struggle certainly seemed to be. Even so, from the footage that preceded the abduction itself, she seemed to share some connection with the man.

Perhaps he was a boyfriend, whom her father might not otherwise have allowed her to marry. Perhaps this pain and humiliation was the price she'd had to pay to marry the man she wanted, without ruining her reputation as a decent girl.

Either that girl had been dragged away unwillingly – or, to keep the respect of her community, she'd had to suffer at their hands. That fact in itself should have been reason enough to stop the brutal practice of marriage by abduction.

In any case, regardless of how that girl might have felt before she was kidnapped, it's likely that she is now married to her abductor – sharing his bed, tending his home, and bearing his children.

I CAN'T GET WITH THAT

I'd seen the way that the Hmong people were treated in Sapa. The Kinh people there were far more affluent and better educated, and many seemed to have little respect for the Hmong, whom they considered dirty and stupid.

My Hmong friends who had studied in Hanoi told me the situation was even worse in the capital. They'd suffered discrimination at the hands of both students and teachers, and hadn't been able to wear their traditional clothing without being mocked and ridiculed.

After the New Year's celebrations, Marinho and I returned to Hanoi, where we had an opportunity to interview one of Vietnam's leading experts on the Hmong people.

Curiously, she herself was Kinh, rather than Hmong.

I would happily elaborate on her long academic

background and the distinguished position she held at an esteemed national institution – but for reasons that will soon become apparent, it's best that she remains anonymous.

While I'd hoped that this expert could give our documentary a firmer academic footing, it quickly became evident that we'd only lose credibility by including her in the film.

Despite living just a few hours' journey from many of Vietnam's Hmong communities, this so-called expert hadn't been to visit any of them – at all – in four or five years. She couldn't even remember how long it had been. She gave a sweetly romanticised account of Hmong culture, and a politically sanitised version of their history. Her attitudes teetered between condescension and outright racism, while the verifiable "facts" she gave were wildly inaccurate.

One of the things that particularly disgusted me was the way this so-called expert described the custom of marriage by abduction.

If a boy and girl liked each other, she said, he'd begin visiting her at night. He'd play a "leaf horn" outside her home and, when the girl heard it, she'd invite him into her bedroom so they could speak together.

I'd never seen a traditional Hmong home that had designated bedrooms – at night, common areas became shared sleeping spaces for entire families. The idea of having individual bedrooms for unmarried children was laughable. Even more ludicrous was the notion that, in such a deeply conservative society, a teenage girl could invite a young man into her bedroom at night.

Yet this "expert" assured me it would happen – not just once, but many times, until the boy and girl fell in love.

I was told that when the couple decided to marry, the boy would come to capture the girl. This was, supposedly, a way of demonstrating the girl's value. The boy and girl would choose the date together, and she'd tell her parents that he was coming to capture her on that day. When he came to take her, the girl's family would pretend to chase him – this was all part of the charade.

The girl would then spend three days in the boy's home, proving to his family that she was hardworking enough to be his bride. If, in those three days, she changed her mind about the boy, she would simply run away and go home. The boy, too, could change his mind and run away if he wanted to, though it wasn't clear where he was supposed to run to. Otherwise, the couple would be married.

This so-called expert painted a lovely picture – but I was looking for facts, not fairy tales. It was incredible to think she was describing the same brutal custom Marinho had captured on video in Sapa.

I pointed out that, in the situation described, the girl was willing to go with the boy. I asked if it ever happened otherwise. The so-called expert simply laughed, and changed the subject.

When I circled back to the question, she conceded that it was possible a boy might capture a girl who didn't like him, but said she was always free to leave. Then she began telling me about the rice cakes the girl's family would receive as engagement gifts.

Ultimately, the interview told me very little about the Hmong people, but it told me a great deal about the level of respect that their community, their culture, and their history was given in Vietnam.

I wasn't sure if this so-called expert was claiming expertise when she was profoundly ignorant, was deliberately spreading lies, or – most likely – a combination of both.

If you asked me to list the true villains in this story, you might be surprised to learn that I wouldn't necessarily include all of the traffickers on that list. I would, however, include this so-called expert, and anyone who stood beside her. Placing ignorance and bigotry in positions of power was a very dangerous thing, and certainly not something Marinho and I would support in any way with our documentary.

IS IT TRUE

The year of the snake was over, and the year of the horse had begun.

After the New Year's celebrations, two new rumours about May began circulating in Sapa.

The first claimed that May had lost contact with her family because they'd begun making plans to rescue her themselves, but hadn't been careful enough. They'd called too often, and May's "husband" had become alerted to their intentions. He'd taken away the phone May had been using, and was now believed to be watching her very closely, leaving her in an even more difficult situation than before.

The second rumour contradicted the first, claiming that May's family hadn't lost contact with May at all. They'd been speaking to her ever since she'd first called from China, six weeks earlier.

This rumour didn't make much sense to me: Blue Dragon had been trying to contact May on the Chinese phone number Zao had passed me. They'd made contact only once, briefly, before the number had stopped working.

If the second rumour was true, May's family must have had a second Chinese number for May – one that actually worked. I'd failed to identify May's kidnappers, and had no other way of finding her. This second Chinese number – if it even existed – was my only hope.

By mid-February, I'd interviewed most of May's closest friends about her disappearance, and it was time to start reaching out to her family.

I'd had a good reason for delaying contact with May's family. I'd known May's friends personally, and counted many of them as friends of my own. It was natural that we would speak together, and that May's abduction would come up in conversation between us.

But I didn't know May's family. We didn't share a common language, and weren't able to converse casually. I'd have to approach them with an interpreter, for the explicit purpose of speaking to them about their daughter's abduction.

This marked a new, more brazen phase of my investigation. When I appeared in May's village and questioned her family on camera, rumours would inevitably begin circulating about my work in Sapa. I'd wanted to delay that moment as long as possible – but now it had arrived.

PICTURES OF YOU

May was the youngest of three sisters.

The middle sister, Cho, was just two years older than May. Cho was the only member of May's family I'd known at all, though only slightly. She had also been kidnapped and sold in China three years earlier.

Dinh, the eldest of the three sisters, was eleven or twelve years older than May. Having married, she now lived with her husband in another village nearby, where she had given birth to three sons.

Before approaching May's parents, I decided to speak with Dinh. We arranged an interview in Sapa, and – as Dinh spoke very little English – Chu offered to interpret for me.

I'd never known Dinh, and couldn't recall ever having met her, but Dinh knew me. She recognised me from a large photograph of May and me which hung on the wall at her parents' house. May must have printed the photograph and given it to her family – I'd never seen it, and hadn't known anything about it.

Dinh showed me another photograph she carried everywhere: a small, laminated picture of her two abducted sisters. The girls stood shoulder to shoulder before a studio backdrop. Their traditional Black Hmong costumes looked very new, and I guessed the photo had been taken during the New Year – most likely in 2011, not long before Cho had disappeared.

May seemed frozen mid-smile, stunned by the flash. Cho – taller and leaner, with a longer face – stared with a cool, unsmiling gaze into the camera.

Dinh bore little resemblance to either of her sisters, and the age difference between them was evident. Dinh was dark and freckled, her fleshy lips hanging open to reveal clusters of crooked teeth. She was adorned with masses of silver jewelry – three bracelets, three rings, three pairs of large hoop earrings, and four silver bands arranged beside a silver comb in her hair.

Despite their age gap, Dinh said she'd been particularly close to May. When May was born, she'd been a sickly child. Dinh had spent a great deal of time taking care of her, and her attachment to May seemed almost maternal.

At the time of her disappearance, May had been renting a room in Sapa – but she didn't like to stay alone, and often slept elsewhere. She frequently stayed with Zao, who rented her own room nearby.

On the night before her disappearance, however, May had stayed overnight with Dinh and her husband in their village. Early the next morning, Dinh's husband had taken both sisters into Sapa on his motorbike, and that was the last time Dinh had seen May. Dinh had followed a group of tourists back to the village, trying to sell them handicrafts, while May had stayed behind in Sapa.

At eleven o'clock that night, Dinh had received a call from Zao, saying that May was gone and was probably already in China.

Dinh relayed the news to her family. Unlike other families whose girls had disappeared, they didn't believe May had been abducted for marriage, but immediately assumed she'd been trafficked to China.

At five o'clock the next morning, Dinh and her parents had gone to Lao Cai with a photograph of May. They'd made many copies of the photo and distributed them widely, but received no response. Returning home, they'd reported May's disappearance to the police in Sapa, and to the government office in their village.

There was nothing more they could do.

Some months later, there had been a message from the government saying that two girls from Vietnam had been found in China. One was dead, but the other was still alive. Families were asked to come and identify the two girls, and to help with the paperwork to bring them home.

Hoping to retrieve their daughter – dead or alive

– May's family had gone to Lao Cai, but neither of the girls had been May.

And then, for two years, there had been only silence.

Dinh said she thought about her sisters all the time, and missed them enormously.

"I think of them when I go to the market," she said. "I see other people's sisters, and I miss them. It's like a bird that was here with me and has now flown away, and I'll never see it again."

When Dinh saw how happy her friends were to spend time with their sisters, she wanted to cry.

When her friends were sad, or upset with their husbands, they all had sisters they could visit and talk to. Dinh wished she could visit her sisters. When her husband was angry with her, he'd tease her about the fact that she had no sisters left, and nowhere she could go. It made her feel terrible.

It was two and a half years since Dinh had last seen May. Was it true that the family had been planning to rescue her from China, and their plan had been discovered by May's "husband"? Was it true that they had a second phone number that still worked, and had been speaking with May all this time? Or was it all just gossip?

The first rumour – that May's family had been planning to rescue her – proved to be small-town nonsense, with no truth in it at all.

The second rumour, however, was confirmed by Dinh. Although she hadn't yet spoken to May directly,

Dinh told me that May was now in regular contact with the family.

May had been forced into marriage with a Han Chinese man. His home was "quite far from Vietnam", and their baby girl was about five months old. May missed her family and friends desperately.

"May – she really want to come back, she cry all day," Chu translated for me. "She say she miss her parents, miss her friends, miss her sister... May – she cry, she just cry, she say she really want to come back here."

Although the details were disturbing, the fact that May was still in contact with her family gave us very real hope. I felt as though we'd been given a second chance.

If I could get May's second Chinese phone number from her family, there might still be a possibility of finding her – and perhaps even of bringing her home.

UNBELIEVABLE

Marinho and I went to meet May's parents in their village. Chan, who'd known the family since she was young, came with us to make introductions, and to interpret for me.

Dinh had helped arrange our meeting. She was waiting for us at the family compound, on the valley wall above the village. The compound lay behind a bamboo gate at the end of a narrow trail between the stepped terraces. Here, chickens pecked at a patch of bare earth between two simple structures of timber and bamboo.

To the Hmong people, the family home had a special significance. It was in this house that May had taken her first breath, as had her brothers and sisters. In accordance with tradition, their placentas had all been buried here.

When a Hmong person died, some clans believed

that their spirit would retrace their steps all the way back to the family home, to reclaim the placenta. Only then could the spirit move on. If the spirit was unable to find its way home, it would be doomed to wander alone forever.

I'd never visited May's home before, and was disheartened to find such a gloomy, desolate place. There was a sense of brooding pessimism that clung to the house, a sense of neglect and decay.

Anyone who has been scuba diving will be familiar with the sensation I felt as I entered the family compound. Descending from the surface of the ocean, the colour gradually leaches out of the world, and is replaced by darkening shades of grey.

There was no question that May's family was poor – yet they hardly seemed any worse off than other families in the same village. While other families I knew had retained a sense of life, here there was a sense of hopelessness, as if the family had simply given up.

Was this the home I hoped to bring May back to? Had it always been such a joyless place? It was difficult to picture such a bright and cheerful girl as May growing up in such grim surroundings, and I imagined the atmosphere had been very different in those days.

May's father Lung was a small man with a narrow, pointed face, protruding teeth, and tufts of black hair sticking out from beneath his dark skullcap. His wife had a colourful scarf tied around her head, and they both wore winter jackets over traditional Hmong outfits.

There was a striking resemblance between Dinh and her mother Dung. They each had the same dark and freckled skin, and the lines of their faces seemed almost identical, framed by their large, silver hoop earrings.

Lung said that he and his wife were both about fifty years old, but they seemed to have aged beyond their years. Their lives had been tough, both physically and emotionally. Within the space of two years, the couple had lost their two youngest daughters to China, and their eldest son to suicide. With Dinh now married into another family, only their youngest son remained of their five grown children.

Aside from the emotional devastation, there had been a more practical dimension to the family's loss. When May and Cho had both been kidnapped from Sapa in 2011, the family had lost much of their income, and had lost the bride prices they would have otherwise received for their daughters. When their eldest son Pao had committed suicide the following year, they'd found themselves with four more mouths to feed.

Pao had been in his late twenties. His wife had borne him four daughters, and had been pregnant with the fifth. Pao had been angry at her supposed failure in not giving him the son he'd wanted. Their marriage had deteriorated until at last Pao had eaten the "poison leaf".

Pao's wife had since remarried, leaving her four eldest daughters behind with Lung and Dung. Pao's brother and his wife also had three daughters, making a total of seven girls in the household. Until the girls were old enough to be married off – or to make their own way selling trinkets in Sapa – they were considered a burden upon the family.

Chan and I sat in the courtyard with Lung and Dung on tiny wooden stools, the only chairs they owned. I didn't suspect May's family of anything, and expected it to be a straightforward interview – but from the very first question, I realised I was wrong. It was an encounter defined by mutual misunderstanding: a collision of two worlds that utterly failed to comprehend each other.

Lung was a suspicious man, and refused to be part of anything he didn't understand. Unfortunately, he didn't seem to understand why I'd come to see him at all. Dung sat silently by his side, making it clear that her husband would speak for both of them.

Chan and Dinh both assured Lung that I'd come to speak with him because I was trying to help May, but that didn't seem to interest him. I could understand Lung's suspicion of us, two foreign men with cameras: we were aliens in his world. But I couldn't understand why he wouldn't encourage any effort to find his daughter, especially as I seemed to be the only one looking for her.

The interview progressed slowly and awkwardly. Lung told me things that made no sense and were simply impossible to believe. He didn't even bother to invent credible fictions – perhaps in his world, I thought, he didn't have to. As the patriarch of the family, perhaps he had no obligation to the truth. Perhaps he needed only to be heard and obeyed.

It was clear that he was hiding something – but what?

Lung contradicted almost everything that Dinh had told me. According to his version of events, the family hadn't gone to Lao Cai the morning after May had disappeared, and hadn't reported her abduction to the authorities. He denied having spoken to May since her abduction, denied having heard anything about her, and denied even owning a phone.

I was confused.

Dinh was standing to one side, listening to our conversation. She clearly disagreed with some of the things her father was saying, but didn't seem to feel it was her place to speak out. Of the two conflicting accounts, I had no doubt that hers was the more accurate.

I said I'd heard that May was now married in China and had a baby there. Lung's utter indifference to my comment suggested either he already knew, or he just didn't care.

I shared several other things I'd learned about May's abduction and her current situation in China. Lung reacted strongly to the suggestion that May had ever had a boyfriend in Sapa, and flatly denied it. Otherwise, his response was always the same – he claimed he didn't know, and showed no interest at all.

I was aware that Lung's life hadn't been an easy one, and I felt a deep sympathy for all he'd been through – but his attitude alarmed me. Was he being wilfully ignorant, rejecting anything that didn't fit neatly into an extremely narrow world view? Or was he deliberately trying to stop me from helping his daughter?

Lung said he'd be happy to see May come home again – yet he seemed to be working to prevent it.

May's second Chinese phone number held our one last hope of finding her. After speaking with May's father, I was convinced that the number existed, and that he possessed it – but he denied any knowledge of it.

I couldn't understand what was happening. What did he want?

A CHANGE IS GONNA COME

After meeting with May's parents, I spoke again with their daughter Dinh.

Apart from May herself, Dinh had been the most sympathetic and understanding member of May's family. I wanted her help to understand what had gone wrong, and how we could fix it. Perhaps she could even get May's second Chinese phone number for me, I thought – but I was too late. Lung had already forbidden Dinh from telling me anything else, and she obeyed him.

Lung was clearly the dominant force in his family. If I wanted May's number, I'd have to find some way to win him over.

We were deep in the labyrinth now, and I could see our prize ahead – almost within reach. The only thing that could help us find May now was that phone number, and the only thing standing between me and that phone number was May's father.

I had to find a way to get that number.

As I reviewed the footage of our interview and tried to understand what had gone wrong, I realised I'd failed to acknowledge one crucial factor: male pride. I was convinced that Lung had been defensive and guarded with me because I'd wounded his pride.

Lung was the uncontested voice of authority in his family. Marinho and I had both been strangers to him. We'd arrived in his home and had physically dominated the space with technologies he could never afford. We'd captured his poverty on camera, for other comparatively wealthy Westerners like ourselves. I'd told him things he hadn't known about his own daughter, slandered May with the suggestion she'd had a boyfriend in Sapa, and claimed that I could help her in ways that he could not.

Without intending to, without even being aware of it, it seemed I'd made Lung feel insecure and inferior in his own home. It was no surprise, then, that he hadn't wanted to share information with me. He'd felt threatened, and had used all his remaining power to spite me.

If I wanted to get May's second Chinese phone number, I'd have to change my approach. Under different circumstances, I suspected that Lung would tell a very different story – and I was right.

Our first meeting had been a major event for the household – a formal interview with Lung and his wife, an interpreter, a cameraperson, two cameras, three microphones, and several family members watching on.

By contrast, I decided to keep our second meeting as simple as possible. Getting at the truth was more important than recording it for our documentary. This time, I didn't take Marinho or any of the equipment – just Chan, to interpret for me.

With the income, experience, and knowledge they gained from tourists, I'd hoped that May and her friends might someday disrupt the established social order, and find a way to escape the extreme male domination they'd been born into.

To my mind, Chan and Lung embodied the two opposing forces in that conflict. Theirs was the clash of the old and new, the oppressors and the oppressed.

Older patriarchs like Lung had wielded so much power for so long they'd become complacent. Young women like Chan stood on the front line of a revolution that was happening right under their very noses.

It was a quiet revolution, a handful of scattered seeds blossoming softly and slowly. These older men were still too blind to see it, too slow to understand what was happening around them. Their world was changing much faster than they realised.

Tourism had struck Sapa like a meteorite. While that impact had in many ways been disruptive and damaging, it had also brought opportunities for the local Hmong women, and allowed the possibility of change.

That change would ultimately be beneficial for everyone. Studies have shown that as women are given more financial power, positive change flows throughout their communities. Men have a tendency to concentrate money and power in their own hands, while women are more likely to share it with others.

Chan was Lung's neighbour, and he'd known her since she'd been a little girl. In recent years, Chan had undoubtedly become Lung's superior in many ways: she was more intelligent, better educated, and had likely already surpassed him in material wealth. She posed a greater threat to the established social order than I ever would – but she was also clever enough to hide that fact.

As an older patriarch, Lung's social position was far superior to Chan's. She treated him with deference and respect, which he accepted as his due. No doubt he saw her as just another local girl of little or no importance.

For the purposes of our second meeting, that was perfect.

As a younger unmarried male, my social position was also lower than Lung's. I'd also have to behave with humility and respect – but not so much that he disregarded me altogether. As a foreigner with no place in Lung's community, it was possible he would dismiss me entirely.

This was the most crucial moment of the entire investigation. Either we walked away with that phone number and a chance of finding May, or we left with nothing. We'd only have one chance – and the greatest danger, I realised, was me.

I had very little respect for Lung, for his wilful

ignorance and barefaced lies. As someone who placed a high value on honesty, I'd never been good with insincerity. I didn't know how long I could feign a respect I didn't feel for Lung.

Could I conceal my true feelings, and keep up the charade long enough to get the phone number we needed?

Or would my conscience kick in, and ruin the entire investigation?

THE UNGUARDED MOMENT

Several weeks after our first meeting with Lung, Chan and I returned to his home in the village. He seemed wary, but agreed to speak with us.

Lung led us inside the family compound. The other family members were nowhere to be seen, and no chairs were offered. The three of us stood and spoke together in the courtyard.

This time, Lung admitted he had spoken to May, and he did have her Chinese phone number – but he refused to give it to me.

Lung told me he didn't trust me, and didn't want my help. Other foreigners had come promising help, he said. They'd never come back, and neither had May.

In any case, he told me, he didn't need or want my help. His family could bring May home themselves if they wanted to, but they didn't want to. Perhaps they might later – but for the moment, he knew she was alive, and that was good enough.

The way he said this last part struck me as particularly cold, and I hoped there was some nuance lost in translation.

Lung's statements were proud but hollow. I was certain he had no intention of ever bringing May home, but I wasn't there to challenge his sincerity: I had to stay focused on getting May's phone number. I took his statements at face value, and played along with his fantasy.

I explained to Lung the benefits of our working together. If he could give me May's phone number, I could pass it to people who could find out exactly where she was. May could then be brought home safely, legally, and at no cost to his family. May's family wouldn't have to risk a long overland journey, and May wouldn't need to hazard an illegal border crossing.

Lung made it clear he wasn't interested in any benefits to May. It was a sickening admission, and a jarring blow to my line of reasoning.

Did Lung really value his ego more than his own daughter? Had I really wounded him so badly he was willing to throw May under the bus?

His attitude reminded me how important this work was. If I could pass May's phone number to Blue Dragon, she could then determine her own future, instead of having it dictated to her by the men in her life.

I changed tack, appealing instead to Lung's sense of

common decency. If he and I worked together with Blue Dragon – "my friends in Hanoi" - there was a very good chance we could catch May's traffickers, and stop them doing the same thing to other girls.

Lung said he didn't care about that. It made no difference to him if other girls were taken – and if he wanted to catch May's traffickers, he would do it by himself.

I was appalled by Lung's stance, and disgusted by his response. The only things he seemed to care about were reasserting his power and reclaiming his lost pride, without giving the least thought to his community or what might happen to his daughter.

Still, I smiled, and treated him respectfully. I asked Chan what he wanted.

"Money," she said. "He wants money."

That knocked me off balance.

May's father seemed to believe that Marinho and I were rich men, and that we were only using May's story to make bags of money for ourselves. He wanted some of that money, and he wanted it now.

I tend to be a reasonable person, and it takes a lot to push me to the edge – but this was too much.

I was well aware that Lung's family was living in poverty, and that their lives could have been easier and more comfortable in many ways, but I couldn't solve all of their problems.

I was doing everything I could to help with what I believed to be the single most horrific problem that plagued Lung's family: the fact that his daughters had been kidnapped and forced into marriage in a foreign country.

Lung had consistently made my work more difficult for me, and now he was trying to blackmail me with my own good intentions. Or else, worse still, he doubted I had any good intentions, and believed I'd come there only to take advantage of his daughter's misery – in which case, he wanted to take advantage of his daughter's misery, too.

I lost all patience with Lung. I asked Chan to relay a message for me, pointing out the fact that Lung was putting his own needs above those of his kidnapped daughter, and what I felt that said about him as a father. I didn't phrase it as delicately as I could have: I had no interest whatsoever in saving Lung's feelings at that point.

It was the only time Chan ever refused to translate a message for me – and, in hindsight, I was grateful that her cooler head prevailed.

"I can't tell him that," she said. "He's my neighbour."

The language barrier between us prevented me from telling Lung what I truly thought of him. I glared at him in a way that would leave no doubt as to my true feelings, and I'm sure he caught the message.

I reminded myself that this man was May's father. As utterly heartless as he seemed to be, he must surely have some feeling towards May, and must also want what was best for her. We'd have to set our differences aside and work together.

I wanted May's phone number, and Lung wanted my money. It was a filthy deal, but if it gave us a chance to help May, then it would be worth it. I swallowed my pride, took a deep breath, and turned back to Chan.

"Okay," I said. "How much does he want?"

I stood waiting while they spoke together in Hmong, and then Chan turned back to me with the bad news.

"He says it's too late. He doesn't want to give you May's phone number."

I'd given Lung a chance to take my money and provide a better life for his family, while allowing me to help his daughter – but I'd also shown him how little respect I truly had for him. Now he refused to deal with me.

Until that moment, it could have been said that Lung was acting in the greater interests of his family. Now he'd chosen his own pride over the well-being of his family – in both Vietnam and China – and he refused to reconsider.

It was the last straw between us.

I'd made plenty of mistakes since I'd begun my search for May – sometimes it felt like I'd made nothing but mistakes – but this was the first time I'd broken something vital which could not be repaired.

Lung and I parted on a bitter note. I was sure that things couldn't get any worse between us – but I was very wrong.

The hostilities had only just begun.

EVERYTHING'S NOT LOST

Despite the damage done between us, I had gleaned two very useful pieces of information from my second meeting with May's father.

With the possible exception of Zao, who had told me nothing, Lung was the only person I'd met who had spoken directly to May. He had a better sense of May's location than anyone else I'd talked to.

When we'd discussed May's potential rescue, Lung had mentioned that May was somewhere very far away, close to the coast. It was at least three days' journey by bus from Sapa, he'd said.

Blue Dragon had dealt with several cases, including Vu's, in which girls had been trafficked thousands of kilometres from Vietnam.

"For the girls, that's the other side of the planet," Michael had told me. "There's no hope that they can escape from so far away."

If Lung's claims were true, May had been taken much further into China than any of the cases Blue Dragon had ever handled – much further than any of the girls I'd spoken to, or even heard about.

China's northern coastline was dominated by the two long jaws that defined the gulf of the Bo Sea. The Chinese capital, Beijing, was sunk deep in the back of the gulf, like a pearl within an oyster.

There were three coastal provinces here – Liaoning, Hebei, and Shandong – plus the special municipalities of Beijing and Tianjin. This region alone was home to a quarter of a billion people: over ten times the entire population of my own country, Australia.

According to the online map I was using, the furthest point of that coastline, on the North Korean border, was forty hours' journey by car from the Lao Cai border crossing. Allowing for slower bus speeds, transfer time, and longer routes between transport hubs, three days' journey by bus could put May anywhere along that northern seaboard.

Is that where my investigation would have led us, if I hadn't bungled the meeting with May's father? Was there any hope left of finding May there?

There was another tidbit of information I'd picked up from my meeting with Lung, too. I'd learned that May hadn't called her father from China – when they'd spoken, he'd called her from Vietnam.

It was a seemingly minor detail that might have been

overlooked, and I was glad I'd caught it. It told me there was one more link in the chain, one more person who'd had possession of May's Chinese phone number.

That person had passed May's number between May in China and her father in Sapa – but who were they, and how could I find them?

If I could answer that question, I might still have a chance to find May.

I SPY

Marinho and I had been conducting most of our interviews at the Yellow Dragon, or at a hotel owned by the family of another Kinh friend.

I'd told Toan and my other friend extremely little about my work, but they trusted me. They knew I'd never had any romantic or sexual involvement with any of the local women, so they hadn't been concerned that Marinho and I had been bringing a series of Hmong girls into their rooms.

After returning from Hanoi, however, Marinho and I found that both hotels were fully booked. We checked into another hotel on Cau May Street, where the owner, Nguyen, didn't know us and had no reason to trust us.

I'd interviewed May's eldest sister Dinh at that hotel, and had then arranged a second interview there – this time, with May's friend Little Chu.

The room we were using had windows on three sides. For the sake of keeping our work secret, it would have been best to shut the door, windows, and curtains completely. As we were relying on natural light for the interview, however, we kept the curtains wide open.

The interview had barely begun when Little Chu was distracted by something moving outside. I turned to look, but it was gone.

Then it happened again – and again.

Someone was creeping around outside the windows, trying to peer inside the room without being seen. We realised it was Nguyen.

Not surprisingly, Nguyen must have found it strange that two foreign men were bringing Hmong women into a closed room. If he'd suspected us of something sexual, he must have quickly realised his doubts were misplaced – but when he saw me interviewing Little Chu, it seemed he'd become even more concerned.

Legally, to film a documentary in Vietnam, Marinho and I were required to obtain journalism visas and a permit from the Ministry of Foreign Affairs. We had to submit in advance a daily shooting schedule with a full list of locations, and a list of all the local people involved in the production. The government would want to know where we'd be going, who we'd be speaking to, and which questions we'd be asking.

Under the terms of the permit, we'd have to be accompanied at all times by a government official, who would ensure there was no deviation from the approved plan. We'd be required to pay his wages and all of his expenses for the full duration of the shoot.

There were high levels of corruption in Vietnam. Marinho and I didn't know if – or how – the authorities might be involved in the trafficking of young women from Sapa. We couldn't reveal the true purpose of our investigation even to my closest friends, and certainly not to the authorities.

Human rights was a sensitive field, and the ethnic minority groups were handled with special care by the government. Even if our application wasn't denied outright, my investigation would be thoroughly crippled by the Vietnamese bureaucracy. My access to the Hmong girls relied on trust and friendship. If the authorities gave me permission to speak to my friends at all, the girls would never speak so freely with a Kinh government official watching over them.

The film permit was charged on a daily basis, encouraging film crews to finish shooting as quickly as possible. Ours was a tiny production, and – for the sake of the girls' safety and our own – it was essential that we spend weeks or months moving slowly and carefully.

Not only would the permit be prohibitively expensive and extremely restrictive, it was simply impossible for a production like ours. There was no way of knowing how long our work might take, or where it might lead us. Flexibility was crucial to the investigation.

If Marinho and I applied for a film permit, were denied, then entered the country on tourist visas, we'd only arouse the suspicions of the Vietnamese authorities. It seemed better not to apply at all – so we didn't.

We were fortunate in the sense that we didn't look like a film crew, and carried very little equipment. With our consumer-level cameras, lightweight tripods, and basic audio equipment, we could simply pass as tourists.

In fact, the entire investigation depended on it.

So far, Marinho and I had been lucky. We'd spent weeks filming around Sapa and its villages, and had never been challenged by the authorities.

Now, this snooping hotel owner could ruin everything for us.

If we were discovered to be shooting a film without a permit, we could be thrown out of the country, and may not be able to return for years. That would bring a sudden end to my investigation, and to any hope of finding May.

Marinho and I had all of our equipment set up and recording inside the room. There was no doubt that Nguyen had seen me interviewing Little Chu.

Was he going to turn us in to the authorities? I didn't know.

Deciding that the best approach was a direct one, I stopped the interview and stepped outside to speak with Nguyen before he slipped away.

But what could I tell him?

Morally, I was certain that trying to find May – and using her story to help protect other girls at risk – was the right thing to do. It also happened to be against the law.

Laws don't change according to individual circumstance, nor are they always moral. On the occasions when laws and morals collide, breaking the law becomes a moral obligation.

I was perfectly comfortable with what I was doing, but I couldn't explain my work to Nguyen, and I certainly couldn't expect any understanding or sympathy from him.

Not trusting myself to lie convincingly, I struggled to find some version of the truth that would fit with what he'd seen already, but wouldn't sound illegal or troubling in any way.

The most crucial thing, I realised, was to act as if the interview was all very innocent and insignificant. If Nguyen understood how much was at stake for us, and how much power he now held over us, he might be tempted to use it.

Nguyen was taken somewhat off-guard when I appeared outside the room. I smiled, as if I was pleasantly surprised to find him there. I wondered aloud if there was anything we could do about the roosters crowing next door, because we were recording video inside the room. I said it as if it were the most natural thing in the world, and not something to hide.

I'd been telling my friends in Sapa that I was making a video about the Hmong people. I had consistently used the word "video", rather than "film" or "documentary". I'd wanted to downplay it, so it seemed like a little project for my own amusement, rather than anything to be taken seriously. Now, I wanted to shift the emphasis even further away from the documentary.

Keeping my tone casual and chatty, I mentioned that I was learning about Hmong culture – which was true, as Little Chu had just been telling me about a local shaman. I mentioned that Little Chu was a friend of mine, and she was helping me out.

Nguyen pretended not to be particularly interested in what we were doing, and soon left. Had he believed my story? I wasn't sure. I decided to continue the interview – it would seem even more suspicious if we stopped recording now.

Little Chu and I spoke for over an hour. Before we'd finished, Nguyen was spotted lurking outside the windows again.

It seemed that my explanation hadn't been enough to satisfy him. Was he planning to report us to the police? Would he ruin my entire investigation?

PRESENCE OF THE LORD

Although she was now eighteen, Little Chu was still small in stature, and appeared more like a child than an adult. She'd been married a year earlier – so far, the first and only one of May's group to have married a local man.

Little Chu had attended only two years of school, but she was an intelligent woman with a clear moral sense. She had no interest in gossip, preferring to stick to the facts.

She told me her husband was a very jealous man, and would be furious if he knew she was meeting with me in a private hotel room, but she felt our cause was important and wanted to help me in any way she could.

Like Marinho and I, Little Chu was doing what she believed was the right thing to do, even though others might consider it wrong.

Little Chu's family had converted to Christianity eleven years earlier. Little Chu's father had been experiencing psychotic episodes whenever he drank alcohol or saw blood. Whenever he'd had to slaughter a pig or buffalo he'd lost his mind, "running and shouting like a tiger", leaping about on all fours. Sometimes he'd run off into the forested mountains, and Little Chu's mother would have to search for him and bring him home.

Whenever he'd been in that state, or whenever he'd been drunk, the family would have to hide the knives. Little Chu's father would show them his hand or leg, and tell them that the meat was ready to eat. He'd tell them to bring him a knife to cut it up, so that everyone could have a piece.

A local shaman had told them that Little Chu's father had been attacked by a vampire in the mountains. If he was left untreated, twelve members of their clan would surely die.

The shaman had performed various rituals for them. He'd told the family they couldn't stay in their house, that they had to move. They'd moved several times, but the problem had persisted, and they didn't know what else to do.

European missionaries had first begun coming to Sapa in the late nineteenth century, and had converted many local families to Christianity. Little Chu's family was told, "If you believe Jesus for sure, nothing will happen to you" – and, in desperation, they'd converted to Christianity.

Three men had come to their home. They'd taken the family altar outside, and stripped the paper offerings from the walls. Carrying out the family's table and chairs, they'd piled everything together and burned it. The family altar had been replaced with an image of Jesus.

Little Chu's father had stopped drinking, and hadn't had any more psychotic episodes.

There was a group of Hmong people in Sapa who identified as Catholics, and a separate group who described themselves as Christians. I asked Little Chu to explain the difference between the two groups.

The only difference, she said, was that the Christians didn't drink alcohol, but the Catholics did. At weddings and funerals, the Christians drank only soft drink.

Neither group permitted their young men to abduct girls for marriage, though their girls were still vulnerable to being kidnapped by the traditional shamanists. If a shamanist man kidnapped a Catholic or Christian girl, her family would generally insist that he convert to her religion before marrying her.

Before May's abduction, May and Little Chu had spent two years living together in a series of rented rooms in Sapa. They'd stopped living together just one month before May's abduction.

Initially, Little Chu told me that she and May had separated because the last room they'd rented together had been too far from the centre of Sapa. Little Chu had wanted to move closer to town, but May had been happy to remain where she was.

When I dug a little deeper, I learned that this was only part of the truth. Little Chu had been reluctant to tell me the real reason, because she didn't want to say anything that might reflect badly on May.

The real reason, she confessed, was because May had started spending time with young men, and had encouraged Little Chu to do the same.

Hmong girls weren't allowed to get involved with young men outside of marriage. As Christians, Little Chu and her family took that prohibition more seriously than some of the other young women did. When Little Chu's mother learned that May had been bringing male friends to their shared room, she'd been furious. At her insistence, Little Chu had moved out.

When I'd spoken to May's friend Xa, she'd struggled to remember what May's kidnapper had called himself – she'd thought perhaps it was Veng.

Little Chu told me it was actually Cheng. She knew for a fact that Zao had also been speaking to Cheng on the phone – she'd overheard them.

Little Chu had been close to May and, after May's abduction, had missed her very much. Certain that May would still remember her phone number, she seemed sad, and a little disappointed, that May hadn't called her from China.

She believed that Zao was now in regular contact with both May and Pang. Little Chu had asked Zao several times for any news of the girls, but Zao had told her very little.

There were so many loose threads leading back to Zao, but still she kept her silence. It would be months before I finally uncovered Zao's secret, and it was a terrible one, but it wasn't at all what I'd imagined.

When the interview was over, I walked Little Chu back to the hotel reception. I said goodbye to her there, before returning to the room to help Marinho pack up the equipment.

Nguyen, behind the desk, smiled and said nothing to me. The moment I was out of sight, however, he pounced on Little Chu. He took her aside and tried to intimidate her, threatening to turn her into the police.

Nguyen wasn't a bad person. He and I were both certain we were doing the right thing – yet we found ourselves on opposing sides of the law, and there could be no real communication between us.

Fortunately, he had nothing to gain by reporting us to the authorities, and the matter ended there. Marinho and I stopped using his hotel for interviews, and soon returned to the Yellow Dragon.

Nguyen's behaviour upset Little Chu, as it was intended to do. As a Hmong woman working in Sapa, it wasn't the first time she'd been mistreated by the Kinh, nor would it be the last.

To her credit, Little Chu's support for my work never wavered.

HAPPY ENDINGS

I'd originally allocated six weeks in Vietnam to investigate May and Pang's disappearances.

By the end of that time, Marinho and I had gathered enough material for a respectable documentary about May, Pang, and the local human trafficking crisis. We had fascinating interviews with Michael, and with most of May and Pang's friends. We had plenty of amazing footage, including the abduction for marriage that Marinho had captured during the New Year's celebrations, and Vu's Chinese wedding DVD.

Our work in Sapa might have ended there – but when Marinho and I realised there might still be a chance of finding May or Pang in China, we decided to remain in Vietnam and learn all that we possibly could.

We had another reason to stay on in Vietnam, too.

When I'd first launched 'The Human, Earth Project',

I'd been influenced by the ideas of renowned journalist Nicholas Kristof. According to Kristof, the type of story that would have the biggest impact was a positive, heartwarming account of triumph about a young, spirited female. People didn't want to listen to the huge, heartrending truths of the world – they wanted to hear stories that were going to make them feel good.

It really didn't matter how good our documentary was, or how important its message might be. All that Marinho and I had uncovered so far was a hopeless, depressing story of greed and violence. Without some kind of happy ending, nobody would want to see it, and it would never make any difference in the world. Everything we were doing would be a pointless waste of time and energy.

I couldn't lie about the human trafficking situation in Sapa and portray it as something it wasn't. But where was I to find a happy ending amongst these mountains of pain and misery? There were plenty of young, spirited females here – but they were living in fear of savage criminals and even their own communities.

It was Michael who gave us a spark of hope. After the New Year's celebrations, Michael had contacted me with some exciting news, and we'd met again in Hanoi to discuss it.

X – Blue Dragon's operative who had rescued Vu, and who had briefly made contact with May – had now succeeded in establishing contact with Pang.

In January, Zao had told me that Pang was happy in

China and planned to stay there, but X had uncovered a very different story: Pang had told him that she wanted to come home.

Blue Dragon had been working to narrow down Pang's location in China, and X was hoping to stage a rescue towards the end of February. There was even a possibility that I could accompany X on the rescue.

It was wonderful to know that Pang would be coming home to her family. It would be amazing to see her again – and to be personally present for her rescue would be phenomenal.

Pang certainly fit the description of a young, spirited female. If we could follow her rescue, return, and reintegration, then Marinho and I would have precisely the kind of story that could make the greatest possible impact against the local human trafficking crisis.

Pang's story would have a happy ending, and so would ours.

It wasn't clear if I'd be able to go with X, and there were concerns that my presence would only complicate his work.

In any case, I immediately applied for and received a dual-entry Chinese visa, and eagerly awaited any further news from Michael. I was ready to leave at a moment's notice.

Given the nature of Blue Dragon's rescue work, their schedule could be highly unpredictable.

In the final week of February, Michael wrote to say they were handling multiple crises at home in Vietnam.

X had been called away to assist the police on a case in central Vietnam, and it seemed unlikely he'd be able to enter China in the coming weeks.

What was more, it had been some time since X had been able to speak to Pang – it seemed that her phone was often switched off for long periods. It wasn't clear whether her captors knew she had the phone, and Blue Dragon had to be very careful communicating with her.

Just three days later, there was another message from Michael. X was racing into China for a particularly urgent and dangerous rescue of a girl who had been sold into a brothel there.

After the rescue, X might have to hurry back to the border with the girl. If at all possible, however, he planned to rescue Pang as part of the same trip.

It was a thrilling moment – Pang could be back in Vietnam in a matter of days! I wouldn't be able to follow X into China, but if all went well, I would join him and the girls on their return across the northern border, and accompany them from there.

The first of March brought an unexpected blow. In Yunnun province, just across the border from Sapa, a group of six men and two women ran into Kunming's central railway station and began attacking passengers with long-bladed knives. Thirty-one people were killed and 143 injured, in an onslaught described as "China's 9/11".

Security clamped down nationwide. X said there were police everywhere, and a heavy military presence.

He succeeded in rescuing the girl from the brothel, but had to abandon any attempt to rescue Pang.

The girl X had rescued told him of other girls in the same brothel who were also in desperate need of assistance. After X got her safely across the border, the Chinese police agreed to accompany him back to the brothel to rescue the other girls.

En route to the brothel, X spoke to the Chinese police about Pang's case. He still hoped to rescue Pang on the same trip, but the police were reluctant to get involved.

When she'd messaged me in Laos, Zao had told me that Pang had two children in China. X hadn't been able to confirm this point – but if it was true, it made Pang's rescue extremely difficult.

If Pang had children, the Chinese police would only allow her to bring them back to Vietnam if she had the consent of her Chinese "husband". For all their years of experience, Blue Dragon had never dealt with a case like this before, and weren't sure how best to handle it.

After the second brothel rescue, X returned to Vietnam several days later than expected – and, within two hours, was called out on another urgent trafficking case in Hanoi. Michael was also called away, on an international case.

Pang would have to wait: nothing else could be done to help her until we learned more.

JOKER AND THE THIEF

I'd already discussed Pang's situation with many of her friends. Now it was time to go out to Pang's village and meet her mother, Bao.

Pang was the fourth of Bao's five daughters, the rest of whom were now married and scattered amongst the nearby villages. Bao – who had been widowed before Pang's abduction – was now living with her only son and his family on the mountainside high above the village.

Marinho, Chan, and I rode out to Bao's village to interview her. She offered to come down and meet us in the valley, to save us the hike up the mountain.

Bao was a small woman with rounded cheekbones and large, expressive eyes. She wore a faded Hmong costume over colourful Western-style clothing, and a bright silver comb shone in her hair. Bao's lack of English couldn't conceal what a genuinely lovely human being she was, and I liked her immediately. Our meeting was the polar opposite of my experience with May's family.

Bao and I found a quiet, picturesque place to speak, above the rice terraces that crowded the valley floor. It was only when we were partway through the interview that the first trekking groups began to appear. Too late, Marinho and I realised we'd set up our cameras beside the main tourist trail that led down into the valley below Sapa.

The trekking groups began arriving more and more frequently, and we had to suspend the interview each time they passed. It became a long, painfully drawn-out process, but Bao accepted each interruption with a gracious smile.

I thought I had a reasonable understanding of Pang's abduction from speaking to her friends, but Bao had some very surprising information for me.

According to Pang's friends, her story had begun like so many others. In late 2010 or early 2011, she'd been contacted by a Hmong man from Bac Ha province, close to the Chinese border. He'd begun calling her regularly.

Over a period of several weeks, Pang had developed feelings for this man she'd never met, and finally he'd come to visit her in Sapa. Pang had no idea, of course, that the young man she was falling for was the leader of a ruthless trafficking ring.

The man had arrived in Sapa with a male friend, three days before Pang's abduction – and that's where her story became very unusual.

I was amazed to learn that the two young men had gone with Pang to meet her mother, and had spent a night at her home in the village. I'd never heard of such audacity amongst the traffickers.

It's easy to see which subgroup a Hmong person belongs to by the design and colouring of their traditional costume. A less obvious but more important distinction in Hmong culture is a person's clan, which is indicated by their family name. Members of the same clan consider themselves brothers and sisters, and support each other as members of a nuclear family do.

Pang's trafficker said he'd come to Sapa to connect with distant members of his own clan, and told Bao that she belonged to his clan. He and his friend were polite, well-mannered young men, and Bao had wanted to make them as comfortable as possible in her home. She'd been so impressed by the young men that in the morning she'd slaughtered a chicken to cook for their breakfast.

There hadn't been so many girls trafficked from Sapa at that time, and Bao struck me as a very trusting person. She never suspected that those two polite young men were watching and waiting for an opportunity to kidnap her daughter. When she said goodbye to Pang that morning, she couldn't have imagined they were seeing each other for the last time.

I pieced together the rest of the story from Pang's friends.

The trafficker had spent time with Pang in Sapa,

buying her meals and a dress, and making her feel special.

One of Pang's friends had been suspicious of this stranger and his sudden displays of affection. She'd asked Pang if she was scared of what the man might do to her. Pang had said no, she wasn't scared. She hadn't been worried at all.

The night before she disappeared, the two young men had taken Pang to dinner in Sapa and pressured her into drinking alcohol. Pang was fifteen, wasn't accustomed to drinking, and had quickly become drunk.

I didn't know if Pang had ever tried alcohol before, but it was clear that she'd never drunk anywhere near as much in a single sitting.

At that time, Pang and her cousin were renting a room together in Sapa. Pang's cousin returned to the room late that evening to find Pang and the young man there together. Pang was "very, very drunk", and had thrown up all over her clothes and bed. Pang's cousin left, and spent the night with a friend.

For the elder generation, the fact that Pang was drunk and alone in her home with a strange young man would have been terribly shameful. Personally, I found it more difficult to understand why Pang's cousin would have left her like that, when it was clear that Pang was not in control of herself or the situation.

In almost all of the later abductions from Sapa, the girls had been taken in the evening and transported under cover of darkness. With the earlier abductions, however, the local communities had been less suspicious, the traffickers had still been fine-tuning their techniques, and many girls had been kidnapped during daylight hours.

It seemed that Pang had been taken early the next day. When her cousin returned to the room that morning, Pang and her trafficker were already gone. Pang's cousin tried to call Pang – and, surprisingly, she got through.

Pang was still in Vietnam – near the border, in Lao Cai – and her phone had not yet been taken from her. Her cousin was very worried about her, and told her to come back.

But Pang didn't want to go back to Sapa. She believed that her trafficker genuinely loved her and wanted to marry her. Pang's cousin asked her if she was scared that the man would take her to China. Even then, on the very brink of disaster, Pang said she wasn't scared. She still refused to believe that the man might traffic her.

Pang's cousin called Bao and told her what she knew. Bao was alarmed, and began making her way into Sapa. It was over an hour's journey by foot and motorbike from her home on the mountainside.

News of Pang's disappearance spread quickly in Sapa. More and more of Pang's friends began calling her, telling her she was making a mistake, urging her to get away from the man and come back to Sapa. Some of them believed the man had used magic to make Pang follow him.

Pang finally seemed to understand what a precarious

situation she was in. She said she was coming back to Sapa – and that was the last anyone heard from her.

Incredibly, the trafficker's friend hadn't yet left town. Pang's cousin had seen him with Pang and her supposed boyfriend the day before, and now she saw him in Sapa's central market. She organised a group of her friends to surround him, and grab hold of him. The girls marched him almost a kilometre by foot – across the square, through the park, and past the lake – to the police station.

By that time, Bao had arrived in Sapa, and she joined the group.

The police questioned the man, but he denied everything. He said he hadn't done anything wrong, and didn't know what his friend had done. In fact, he said they weren't really friends, they'd only just met in Sapa three days earlier. He said he had no idea what had happened to Pang.

The police didn't know what to do with the man, and let him go. The girls were furious at how little the police seemed to care about their friend's kidnapping.

The police thought perhaps Pang had been abducted for marriage. They told Bao to go home and, if she didn't hear anything from Pang, to come back in two or three days. Only then would they start looking for her daughter.

MOTHER MOTHER

Bao hadn't been aware of any romantic connection between Pang and her kidnapper. When she heard that Pang seemed to have gone willingly with the man, however, she thought perhaps it really was an abduction for marriage.

The man knew where Bao lived. If he'd kidnapped her daughter for marriage, his family would soon come and speak with her at her home in the village – so she went back home, and she waited.

They never came, and nobody knew what had happened to Pang.

Every day for a week, Bao tried calling Pang's number. If Pang was still in Vietnam, she reasoned, her phone number would still work – but it didn't.

As the days dragged past, Bao realised the utter helplessness of her situation. She had no idea what was happening to Pang, where she might be, or even if she was still alive. Bao had nobody to help her, and she felt very alone.

Every day, she said, she just stayed home and cried, and wished there was something she could do to help her daughter. Later, there were times she went to Sapa and saw Pang's friends, or the corner where Pang used to work, and she missed her daughter terribly.

Up until that time, there hadn't been many girls being trafficked into China from Sapa, but Bao soon began to hear of girls disappearing in much greater numbers. What could any of their families do about it? China was such a vast country, and once a girl had been taken, it seemed impossible to find her again.

The days became weeks, then months, and years. Bao was certain of only one thing: that Pang would never come home again.

After almost three years, another of Bao's daughters had given her a piece of paper with an unfamiliar phone number. The daughter said she'd received it from another girl from their village, who had received it from her boyfriend, who had received it from his schoolteacher in Lao Cai.

The phone number was Chinese. Bao's daughter wasn't sure, but she'd been told that it might be Pang's.

Bao didn't know what to believe. Many girls had been taken by that time, including others with the same name.

She rang the number, and an unfamiliar voice

responded. It was a young woman with a strange accent who claimed to be her daughter. Bao didn't believe her – the voice was very different to Pang's, and was difficult to understand – but the young woman insisted.

To test her, Bao began asking the young woman all kinds of questions about her family. Only when she'd answered all of the questions correctly did Bao realise she was in fact speaking to her own daughter.

Bao began to weep. She told Pang she'd never expected to hear from her again, and had thought she was already dead.

Pang told her not to cry – she hadn't died yet. One day she'd come home to Sapa, she said.

To Bao, that was almost too much to hope for. She would have loved to see Pang again, but it seemed impossible.

Bao had so many questions she wanted to ask Pang, and so did I – but right now, there was only one question that really mattered: Had Pang given birth in China?

Strangely, there was a great deal of confusion over the number of children Pang had in China – whether it was one, two, or three – but there was no doubt that she was now a mother.

Bao believed that Pang had two children: one was almost two years old, and the other had been born just four months earlier. Other sources differed, for reasons that later became clear.

In terms of her rescue, it made little difference exactly how many children Pang had. The Chinese police had made it clear that Pang couldn't bring any of her children home without the knowledge and consent of her "husband".

This was a man who had bought and raped Pang, for the express purpose of having children. Needless to say, there was absolutely no chance that this man would now give Pang permission to take his children away from him – nor would he allow Pang herself to leave.

Even if Blue Dragon could rescue Pang, they couldn't legally bring her children back across the border. To take a Chinese child away from its Chinese father would be a legal nightmare, Michael said – especially for a foreign woman with no legal status in China.

Pang was still a teenager, barely more than a child herself. She now found herself with a heartbreaking dilemma that no mother should ever have to face: the choice between her children and her own freedom.

Would she spend her life in China, in the hands of a man she hated, for the sake of her children? Or would she abandon her children, so that she could return home to her family in Vietnam?

Or could we find some other solution for Pang, even if it meant breaking the law?

EVERYBODY'S TALKIN'

I was curious to know how Pang had been able to pass her phone number back to her mother in Sapa. It was a bizarre story and took some digging, but I was finally able to piece it together.

Almost three years after she'd been trafficked from Vietnam, Pang had been able to access a phone in China. She'd desperately wanted to call home and speak to her mother – but by that time, she couldn't remember any Vietnamese phone numbers.

Pang's Chinese "husband" had remained in contact with the middleman who'd sold him his teenage bride. The middleman put Pang in touch with another Vietnamese Hmong woman he had sold into marriage in China.

The other woman had been in China since 2010, and had already succeeded in making contact with her own family in Vietnam. Her brother worked as a teacher in Lao Cai, and Pang asked for his number.

Pang then called the brother, and said she needed his help to contact her own family. She'd never even had a chance to say goodbye to her mother, and hadn't spoken to her for almost three years. She wanted to know how her family was, and wanted them to know she was still alive.

The brother agreed to help find Pang's mother. Pang told him as much detail about her family as she could. She told him how many people were in her family, and their names. She told him the name of the village, and the approximate location of her mother's home.

There are no street names or numbers in the villages – just a web of narrow pathways snaking out between the homes and fields. With so many people sharing names that are the same or very similar, it can be surprisingly difficult for an outsider to locate someone there.

Pang's number was passed from hand to hand, until at last it found its way to her mother in the village.

I was intrigued. One of the first things the traffickers did was to cut their victims off from all communication. This was necessary for the traffickers' own protection. Why would the middleman then connect their victims with each other?

The answer remains a mystery, and I can only speculate. By giving Pang a friend who could empathise with her current situation and speak to her in her own language, perhaps the traffickers hoped to ease her loneliness, to make her more cooperative and less likely to run away.

If that friend had already accepted her new life in China, submitting to her "husband" and bearing his children without fuss, then perhaps the traffickers thought she'd be a calming influence on a more defiant girl like Pang.

Had Pang been able to speak to anyone else in China?

I discovered that Pang was now connected to a network of ten or twelve Vietnamese Hmong women – including three from Sapa – who spoke regularly with one another. All of the women had been trafficked and forced into "marriage"; most of them had been in China for several years, and already had children in China. Nearly all of these women now seemed resigned to spending the remainder of their lives in China with the men who'd bought them.

Pang, it seemed, had never accepted her Chinese "marriage". Even now – after almost three years of "marriage", and perhaps two years of motherhood – it seemed that Pang was still rebelling furiously against her "husband", and making life very difficult for him.

I imagined Pang's "husband" calling the middleman in frustration and despair, worried that his "wife" might run away – and angry too, perhaps, that he hadn't received the compliant young woman he'd thought he was paying for.

I could imagine the middleman passing him the phone numbers of other trafficked women who already seemed to have accepted the restrictions and deprivations of their new lives, in the hope that they would help settle Pang.

I understood that the middleman would want Pang's "marriage" to succeed. His clients knew where he lived and how he made his money, and this knowledge gave them a certain power over him.

An enraged client could easily report him to the police, and could supply enough evidence to have him sent to prison. It was in the middleman's best interests to peddle a satisfactory product, to keep his customers happy.

Even so, it was difficult to understand why a middleman would expose his network to one of its victims. The risks seemed to outweigh the benefits – especially when it came to someone so unpredictable as Pang.

Sometimes Pang's "husband" became angry that she was spending too much time and money on the phone. In one month, Pang's phone bill would cost him 700 yuan ($105) or more – a considerable expense in China. He often complained, in the hopes that she would stop making so many phonecalls, but still he let her keep the phone.

Knowing Pang and how merciless she could be when she was upset, I could easily believe that her "husband" – who had given Pang every reason to be angry – was genuinely frightened of his "wife" and what she might do.

Pang was a very emotional person, who rarely seemed to think through the consequences of her actions. I secretly cheered her resistance, and was glad that she'd been able to keep some small measure of autonomy.

At the same time, however, I was aware that Pang's "husband" still controlled all of the crucial aspects of her life. There was a very real possibility that Pang's unrestrained behaviour could expose her to dangers greater than any she'd yet experienced, or even imagined.

Pang was a saleable commodity. If she pushed her "husband" too far, she could easily be resold for marriage, for prostitution, or even for her organs.

At one stage, the middleman had put Pang in contact with another trafficked girl that she'd known personally. The two girls had once been imprisoned together in the middleman's house. The middleman told the girls that they'd both been sold to men from the same region, and were now living very close to each other.

Pang had relentlessly irritated her "husband" for several months, until at last he'd given in. He'd taken her to visit the other girl so that they could speak in person.

I was amazed. I'd never heard of anything like it before – but the biggest surprise was yet to come.

Just a few weeks earlier, Pang had received a call from an unknown number. Like her mother, at first she hadn't recognised the voice on the other end of the line. It was a voice she'd known since she was a child, but hadn't heard in years.

That voice was May's.

May had been put in contact with a trafficked woman from Sapa who had been in China for eight years and had many contacts there. The woman said she'd heard of another trafficked girl named Pang who had come from May's village. May had asked for Pang's number, called it, and the two friends were able to speak for the first time in almost three years.

Pang herself had never spoken to the other woman, and didn't know who she was: Pang's phone number had been passed beyond her own network.

Unfortunately, May and Pang had little opportunity to speak. May had just given birth to her first child, a little girl. Her daughter was sickly, cried constantly, and demanded a great deal of attention.

May wanted to speak to her own mother. She remembered her parents' phone number but wasn't able to call it, and didn't know why. She asked for Pang's help, just as Pang had asked for help from the teacher in Lao Cai.

It was Pang who had passed May's number back to May's family in Sapa. Pang had given it to her mother, who had given it to May's parents.

I had the answer I needed. Bao was the mysterious connection, the missing link between May in China and May's family in Vietnam.

I asked Bao if she would give me May's Chinese number, and she was happy to do so. She took out her phone – a cheap, older model, which predated smartphones – and began clicking through the menus.

It was a thrilling moment. Apart from May's own family, who wouldn't give me the number, and perhaps Zao, who wouldn't even speak to me, nobody else in Sapa seemed to have May's number. At last, I'd found someone who was both willing and able to give it to me. This could be the turning point of my investigation.

Bao put her phone down, her face marked by concern. I asked Chan what was wrong.

"She says she's sorry," said Chan. "But she doesn't have the number anymore."

CALL IT WHAT YOU WANT

In early March, after Marinho and I had spent our first two months in Vietnam, our visas expired and we'd had to leave the country.

Marinho and I still hadn't finished our search for the other 99 local people I'd photographed on my first journey through Asia. While that search seemed senseless to me now, I'd already committed to it, and intended to honour that commitment.

Our visa run gave us an opportunity to search for three children in Cambodia we'd skipped over when we'd come rushing directly from Laos to Vietnam in early January. After making the long journey south, Marinho and I succeeded in finding all three of those children amongst the scattered ruins of Angkor Wat.

It was the first chance I'd had to step away from my investigation, and to reflect on all I'd seen and heard over the past two months. Marinho and I now had plenty of material for our documentary – but we didn't yet have a title for the film.

I thought of May, her sister Cho, and the other kidnapped girls she'd considered her sisters – Vu, Pang, and Shu. Each of them had been betrayed, stolen, and sold, along with countless other sisters and daughters from Sapa.

I could think of only one title that seemed to encapsulate the story we were still uncovering. I decided to write it out by hand, as I had with the name of 'The Human, Earth Project'.

This time, however, all I had was a scratchy old felt-tipped marker and a camera – not even a scanner to capture the image properly. I wrote "SISTERS FOR SALE" on a piece of scrap paper, photographed it, and it became the label that has stuck to my work ever since.

A few days later, Marinho and I returned across the border for one final, intense month in Vietnam – a month that very nearly tore the project apart.

HERO

Vietnam's capital is Hanoi, in the north – but its most populous city is Ho Chi Minh City, over a thousand kilometres to the south. Ho Chi Minh City had been the capital of South Vietnam during the war, when it was known as Saigon.

Ho Chi Minh City was a steamy modern metropolis swarming with a turmoil typical of Southeast Asia. Overhead, gleaming towers of steel, glass, and concrete thrust themselves up into the sunlight. Lower down, thick black tangles of electrical cables amassed over shadowy canyons reverberating with the ceaseless howl of motorbikes.

Here, a Frenchman named Georges Blanchard had been waging his own war against human trafficking for the past nineteen years.

Georges was the founder of Vietnam's original

counter-trafficking organisation, Alliance Anti-Trafic, which now operated across Southeast Asia. A warm, friendly man in his early fifties, Georges had invited me to his office in the city, and agreed to share his experiences with me.

It had been ten weeks since I'd met Michael Brosowski, founder of Blue Dragon Children's Foundation, in Hanoi. Georges and Michael were fighting the same war at opposite ends of the same country, but the contrast between the two men was striking.

Michael was tall and slim. He spoke in a calm and measured way, and dressed in business attire. His organisation – housed in bright, spacious offices – seemed to have taken on an independent life of its own, and gave the impression of a well-oiled machine.

Georges, on the other hand, was a shorter, stockier man with twinkling eyes and a ready laugh. He dressed more casually, spoke with great passion, and seemed inseparably tied to his organisation. Alliance Anti-Trafic was housed in a small, dark, temporary space, with the clamour of construction next door.

There was no question that Georges and Michael both had a profound and very genuine commitment to fighting human trafficking. Both had done and continue to do phenomenal work, and I have enormous admiration for each of them.

Over the coming months, I would be working most closely with Michael, a fellow Australian whose work was also centred on northern Vietnam – yet somehow

I found myself empathising more with Georges, a foreigner with whom it could be a challenge even to communicate.

Michael's organisation represented a polished ideal, while Georges' represented an unvarnished reality I was much more familiar with. While Michael was a captain in command of his vessel, Georges was labouring over the oars, battling his way across the waves.

At a glance, it was clear that Georges and his staff were fighting for something they truly believed in. Their work seemed neither easy nor comfortable, yet they pushed on regardless.

In many ways, Georges reminded me of myself – an idealist and an underdog who didn't always have the resources he needed, who would forge ahead on pure determination when times were tough. I saw Georges' struggle in my own.

Funnily enough, I later learned that Georges and I had both been born on the same day, twenty years apart. Though I had little interest in astrology, we both seemed to be very typical Pisces – artistic, idealistic, and deeply empathetic.

As a child, Georges had lived in northeastern France, close to the German border. He recalled the dark-haired, dark-eyed children who had first begun arriving at his school in 1972, as refugees from the Vietnam War.

In a region of blonde hair and blue eyes, the appearance of these children had struck Georges as "something magical", and had left a deep and lasting impression upon him. Then just ten years old, Georges began to take an interest in any news from Vietnam. He told himself that if he ever had a chance to take a flight somewhere, he'd go to see the distant land from which these children had come.

Georges had been just fourteen when his family had fallen apart, and he'd spent the next four years living in a Paris brothel while undertaking an apprenticeship. When at last he'd had the chance to take that flight, he'd gone directly to Vietnam, and had been living there ever since.

Georges had begun fighting human trafficking in Vietnam even before the issue had been officially recognised there. When in 1995 he'd launched his first project to protect Vietnamese children from the predations of sex tourists, the Vietnamese government had refused to acknowledge the issues of prostitution and human trafficking. For years, Georges had been forced to work behind a veil of secrecy.

In 2001, as perceptions began to change, Georges had formalised Alliance Anti-Trafic to combat sex trafficking networks. The organisation now worked with governments, police forces, and likeminded organisations across Southeast Asia.

When I met him in March 2014, Georges had been living in and around Ho Chi Minh City for more than half his life. His wife and children were Vietnamese, and he spoke the language fluently.

Georges was much more comfortable speaking

French or Vietnamese than he was speaking English. Ours was an unusual interview – I'd ask a question in English, Georges would respond in French, then he'd provide a brief approximation of his answer in English so that I could follow up with further questions.

It wasn't until months later, after our footage had been properly translated into English, that I understood everything that Georges had told me.

When it came to cross-border trafficking, different countries played different roles. There were source countries, transit countries, destination countries, and countries that combined these roles in various ways.

Vietnam was primarily a source country – with its large but youthful population, Georges said, it was a "gold mine" for traffickers.

While Alliance Anti-Trafic also assisted men and boys who had been enslaved and forced into manual labour, their core work was helping victims of sexual exploitation, who were predominantly female. The organisation had repatriated Vietnamese sex trafficking survivors from twenty-two countries across Asia and the world.

Malaysia was a major regional transit hub, Georges said, with Vietnamese girls passing through on their way to locations as diverse as North America, Europe, Russia, Australia, Africa, and other parts of Asia.

Because they were nearly always trafficked by deception, Georges told me that "99%" of victims would go to the airport and fly by themselves, not realising they'd be landing in a trap that had been carefully prepared ahead of time.

On arrival in her destination country, a victim's documents would be seized, and she would find herself stuck in a foreign land with no support. The traffickers would often use threats against both the woman and her family to bend her to their will.

Debt bondage was extremely common: the traffickers would demand repayment for travel expenses and agency fees, in addition to ongoing food and accommodation costs – plus interest. These debts were structured in such a way that a victim would not be able to earn her freedom for years, if at all.

"The trafficker will say, 'If you don't repay your debt, I'll take your little sister,' or, 'Your family will face the consequences'," Georges told me. "So the system traps the girl – she can't change her mind."

Sometimes the traffickers were family networks, and sometimes they were larger international mafias supplying the major prostitution centres, like those in Hong Kong and Macau.

Interestingly, the smaller local networks had one powerful advantage over the larger mafias: they were in the best position to build trust with their victims.

By far the majority of girls that Alliance Anti-Trafic had repatriated from China said they had first been approached by a family member, a close friend, or a neighbour from their own village. In each case, the initial contact was made by someone the girl knew and trusted.

One of the greatest challenges Alliance Anti-Trafic faced was one I'd also recognised in Sapa – the difficulty of reintegrating a survivor into a community where the standard of living was low and her options were limited. The organisation would work closely with the family, community, and the local authorities to bring a sense of stability and purpose back into a woman's life.

Alliance Anti-Trafic ensured that survivors had the legal, medical, and psychological support they needed, as well as any specialised assistance they may require.

According to the policies the organisation had developed, they monitored each survivor for a full two years after her return. In reality, however, Georges said they maintained some level of contact with every one of the thousands of survivors they'd assisted since 1998.

I thought of May and Pang. Even if we were able to find them and bring them home to their families in Vietnam, that wouldn't be the end of their journey – far from it. Once a girl had been taken, her life became far more complex, and would never be the same again.

While Alliance Anti-Trafic spent a great deal of time and energy reintegrating survivors, Georges made it clear that this was not the organisation's true focus. Alliance Anti-Trafic conducted personal investigations, ran awareness programs, and helped to develop new laws and regulations so that they could help prevent trafficking on the individual, community, and national levels.

"The real goal is not to save one girl," Georges said. "She's already a victim. The goal is to prevent other victims."

HIGH AND DRY

Behind the smiles and laughter, something was clearly upsetting Georges.

I wondered what it would take to upset someone who had worked so closely with such horrific things, for so many years – but I didn't have to wonder very long. When I found out what it was, it upset me, too.

While all of the experts agreed that human trafficking was a colossal problem, none of them could agree just how big it was.

In 2005, the United Nations' International Labour Organisation estimated that 12.3 million people were victims of various forms of slavery around the world.

Seven years later, they increased that figure to 21 million victims, with more than half of these in the Asia-Pacific region. They estimated that 98% of all commercial sex trafficking victims were girls and women.

In 1999, scholar Kevin Bales had given 27 million as his best estimate. Some activists, he claimed, gave a range as high as 200 million victims.

Walk Free's inaugural Global Slavery Index had given an estimate of 29.8 million victims in 2013. This figure would be revised upwards to 35.8 million the very next year, and 40.3 million by 2016. Over two-thirds of victims were claimed to be female, and 15.4 million were said to be in forced marriages.

One of the reasons for these wildly divergent figures was that it was very difficult to say exactly what human trafficking was. Internationally, there were many conflicting definitions of human trafficking, and a great deal of confusion about what the term actually referred to. The most prominent definition, formulated by the United Nations in 2000, was a long and complex one. The waters were further muddied by competing terms, such as "modern-day slavery".

The real problem, however, was that these numbers were being given as measurements for something that was essentially immeasurable. Victims of human trafficking were, by their very nature, voiceless, and generally hidden from view. Trying to count them was like trying to count the number of fossils concealed below ground.

After nineteen years fighting on the front lines, Georges felt it was impossible to provide such statistics with any measure of accuracy, and somewhat arrogant even to try.

In any case, it was clear that the figures were beyond all comprehension. At that time, the entire population of my country, Australia, was only 23 million people. It was impossible for me to grasp the individual suffering of twenty, thirty, or forty million human beings.

For many people, the term "slavery" is associated most strongly with the transatlantic slave trade, in which some twelve million Africans were brought to the Americas over the course of four centuries. Unknown millions also died in Africa, in the Caribbean, and en route as part of that trade – yet all estimates suggest that more people are living in slavery now than at any other point in history.

While Georges was reluctant to discuss the numbers, he did tell me that more and more people in Vietnam seemed to be falling victim to human trafficking each year. Michael had said the same thing in Hanoi, and it was a sentiment I'd heard echoed repeatedly in Sapa. The statistics, however flawed they might be, appeared to confirm this trend on a global level.

Human trafficking was a horror of inconceiveable proportions, which only seemed to be growing with each passing year. Its shadow fell, to various degrees and for various reasons, over every country on Earth.

The most widely respected report on the subject was the Trafficking In Persons (TIP) Report, issued annually by the US State Department.

The TIP report rated each country on a three-tier system, where Tier 1 denoted the countries that were combatting human trafficking most effectively, and Tier 3 those who were failing. Most countries were placed somewhere in between – either on Tier 2 or, worse still, on the Tier 2 watchlist.

In 2012, Vietnam had been promoted to Tier 2 from the watchlist. On the surface, this seemed to be good news, but Georges was furious.

For a government, being upgraded on the TIP report conferred status in the international community, while being downgraded carried a mark of shame.

As such, Georges believed that the report was used as a political tool and was often biased, measuring not only a country's performance against human trafficking, but also how friendly their relationship was with the US government at that particular time.

It seemed that the Vietnamese government had won political approval from the United States – but, behind the scenes, this had been devastating for Alliance Anti-Trafic.

On the basis of the TIP report, it seemed the funding bodies behind Alliance Anti-Trafic believed that Vietnam's human trafficking problem was no longer so serious. In just one year, the organisation's funding had been slashed from $400,000 to just $100,000.

Alliance Anti-Trafic had already been fighting an uphill battle against human trafficking – and now they'd had the legs cut out from under them. They were struggling against an ever-growing crisis with just one quarter of their previous funding. Not only had they been forced to close their women's shelter and abandon much of their work, it was impossible for them to implement long-term plans with a budget so tight, and with future funding so uncertain.

Georges had the knowledge, experience, and passion to lead a sustained campaign against human trafficking. He'd spent almost two decades putting the right people and processes in place, building the necessary relationships in Vietnam and beyond.

It was people like Georges who could most help protect vulnerable communities like those in Sapa. I'd seen the desperate need for this kind of work, and what a huge difference it could make. I'd also seen how much more could be done, with the right support.

Now, while the traffickers gathered ever-more victims, Georges and Alliance Anti-Trafic had been left high and dry. They were like a company of soldiers who were being sent into battle without ammunition. It was a terrible blow to exposed communities, and a devastating victory for those who would exploit them.

HOPE AND VALIDATION

While my own work and funding goals were far more modest, I'd also found myself in a difficult position financially, and knew how frustrating fundraising could be.

After our final month in Vietnam, Marinho and I would enter China – but it still wasn't clear if we'd have enough money to continue our work there.

We'd launched a fundraising campaign soon after our arrival in Vietnam. Thanks to its organisers John and Barry, and the support of dozens of bloggers around the world, the campaign had received plenty of attention – but we still hadn't received the support we needed.

A Dutch friend had secretly raised over $500 on our behalf, which she'd contributed to the campaign immediately after it first opened in late January. Since then, the campaign had been highly unpredictable: on some days we received hundreds of dollars, while on others we received only ten or twenty dollars.

Often, despite keeping our costs to a bare minimum, money was gushing out of the project far more quickly than it was coming in. We weren't receiving enough to sustain our immediate needs, much less the continuation of our work in China, where our costs would be significantly higher.

We'd given ourselves one month to raise $12,000. When the month was over, we hadn't even raised half of that amount.

Our campaign was being hosted on a fundraising platform which did not normally allow extensions. Just a few days before the end of the month, however, the hosts reached out to us with a special invitation.

For International Women's Day in early March, they were promoting a series of campaigns that supported women's rights. They offered to extend our campaign so that we could participate, and we gratefully accepted. We were given an extra month to raise the funds we needed.

When I wasn't busy with the investigation, I spent my time sending out thousands of personal messages. Few of those messages were ever answered, and I'm sure that most were never read. It was exhausting, and I felt as though I was beating my head against a wall.

And then, at the beginning of March, a complete stranger from the other side of the world gave us $1,100 to continue our work. It was, by far, the largest single contribution we had ever received. I was humbled by this act of generosity, and far more so when I discovered the circumstances surrounding it.

The stranger, I learned, was a 23-year-old named Myste, from Pittsburgh. In addition to working multiple jobs, Myste was taking care of her sick mother, and struggling to maintain her crumbling family home. The money that Myste had contributed to our work was the inheritance she'd received from her grandmother, who had recently passed away.

Myste said that giving that money to support our work was the greatest thing she'd ever done, and she has been closely involved with the project ever since. Two years later, Myste was to play a far greater role in saving the 'Sisters for Sale' documentary, and was rightfully credited as the film's executive producer.

In a practical sense, Myste's contribution made a very real difference to our work – but it also meant a lot to me personally. It was gratifying to see our work reaching people around the world who believed in us and our cause, and who were willing to support us in a meaningful way.

Ultimately, our campaign was supported by hundreds of people from five continents, and we just reached our $12,000 goal.

At last, Marinho and I had the money we needed to go to China – but we still didn't have May's Chinese phone number, and there was a far darker storm brewing on the horizon.

UNDERDOG

My brother Nick is two years older than I am.

When we were young, he'd been my superior in every way. He'd been bigger, stronger, smarter, and faster.

From an early age, I'd felt as if Nick and I were in competition with each other, and it was a competition I could never hope to win. If I was quick and clever, I might occasionally snatch some fleeting victory. Otherwise, I spent my childhood feeling as though I was getting the small half of everything, so to speak.

It was an accident of birth, that was all. My brother just happened to have been born first, a fact which shaped my daily reality.

I didn't really want to win any competition against my brother – I didn't really want to compete at all. I only wanted what was fair. It was a feeling that left me with a burning hunger for justice, which became a fundamental part of me.

When I grew up and began to understand more of the world I realised that, in reality, my brother and I were both incredibly fortunate. As white, middle-class males in a developed nation, we had both been winners in the lottery of birth.

I had in fact been born with the big half of everything; I'd just never realised it.

My hunger for justice was not diminished with that revelation – it only grew. I knew how it felt to get the small half, and I didn't want anyone else to feel that way. I'd done nothing to deserve the comparatively easy life I'd been born into, while so many others were suffering around me. I wanted to help balance the scales for those who had been born less fortunate.

Marinho had a similar hunger for justice, which burned even more fiercely than my own. This seemed to be the true reason he'd agreed to accompany me on such a long, gruelling, and dangerous journey with so little hope of success, for so little personal reward.

Neither Marinho nor I was being paid for our work with the project. In lieu of payment, I'd offered Marinho an equal share in the documentary and some of the film equipment to keep, in addition to covering all of his food, accommodation, and travel costs.

Part of the reason the project had appealed to Marinho is that it offered him an all-expenses-paid trip through ten countries of Asia, most of which he'd never been to. He was a passionate photographer, and the project gave him a chance to explore his craft in a wide range of new environments. It was an opportunity he'd relished, taking tens of thousands of photographs with which he hoped to build his name.

I had great respect and admiration for Marinho, and the project would have been impossible without him. He was a fighter, and a damned good one – he was clever, courageous, and uncomplaining.

It made an enormous difference knowing I had the support and encouragement of someone who not only shared my beliefs, but who was also willing to go to extremes for them.

Marinho had been far more than just a cameraperson. With everything we were going through, it meant a lot to me just knowing I wasn't alone. A great deal of my strength and courage came from having Marinho there at my side, and I don't know how far I could have gone by myself.

Although we never discussed it, I suspected that Marinho's hunger for justice was rooted in a childhood experience somewhat similar to my own. Judging by the depth of his passion, however, it seemed that Marinho had suffered injustices far worse than any I'd experienced.

I had the impression that he'd spent his childhood fighting against a much more formidable opponent – a father figure, perhaps – against whom he could never hope to snatch even a fleeting victory. Someone who'd allowed him neither the big nor small half, merely the crumbs.

That experience seemed to have left Marinho not only with a burning hunger for justice, but also a deep distrust of any form of authority.

There seemed to be a doomed, tragic sense to Marinho's struggle. To him, the only fights that were truly worth fighting seemed to be self-destructive ones, in which the odds were stacked almost impossibly high against him. He struck me as a David in constant search of a Goliath.

I was a peacemaker by nature, and had never enjoyed fighting. I fought only when I felt it was truly necessary, when my hunger for justice demanded it. I saw fighting as a means to an end and, when it was over, I wanted a quiet life.

For Marinho, it seemed that the fighting was never over. There was a rebellious streak in him a mile wide, and he seemed to relish and find purpose in the fight itself. His childhood had made him strong, but I was sure it hadn't been an easy time for him. He was willing to go to extremes for even the most negligible gain, or the smallest moral victory – especially when there was a uniform or figure of authority involved.

He seemed cursed to a restless, warrior's life, determined to fight until his last breath, with no hope of peace until he realised the only true battle was within him.

Marinho had once told me that, after his work with the project was over, he didn't want to go back to live in his own country. "Only to start the revolution," he'd said with a smile at the corner of his lips, in a way that might or might not have been a joke.

There was much to Marinho that I didn't understand – why he concealed his identity with multiple aliases, for example – but there was no doubting his courage and intelligence.

He'd told me how he'd been mugged one night by a gang of knife-wielding thieves in a large city in southern Europe, where he had been living at the time. Rather than allowing them to take the valuable camera he'd been carrying, Marinho had managed to convince the thieves – in a second language – to take an empty, useless bank card from his wallet. He'd assured them there was plenty of money on the card. The thieves had told him that if he was lying and they ever saw him again, they'd kill him. Marinho changed his facial hair, began walking a different route through that part of the city, and went on with his life.

Any incident that left him feeling powerless in the face of authority, however, seemed to shake Marinho deeply.

Since the beginning of our journey together, Marinho had been involved in several unwanted encounters with the police, the military, and immigration officials. He'd been able to talk his way out of most of these situations, as he had with the traffic police in Vientiane.

During the Lunar New Year, however, Marinho and I had been invited to spend an evening with Huong's family in her village. The next morning – still half-asleep, and somewhat hungover – we were packed onto the back of motorcycles, driven into town, and shepherded inside a small building. When Marinho suddenly realised he was inside a police station surrounded by uniformed officers, he froze, and turned pale.

"Toan is the betrayer," he muttered, and seemed incapable of saying much else.

I didn't understand the situation either, but was confident that Toan would never betray us, and I wasn't worried. I found Marinho's response funny, but he didn't see any humour in the situation. He seemed like a man on the gallows, with the noose already tightening around his neck.

As foreigners, Marinho and I had been legally required to register our presence in Huong's village, and her family felt it was best if we complied. A few minutes later we were free to go – but it seemed to take Marinho some time to recover from the incident.

Marinho was a highly intelligent human being with a deep capacity for thought and feeling. Externally, he was a large, physically formidable man – but within him there seemed to be a child who had suffered greatly, and was suffering still. Like all of us, he was struggling to find his way in a complex and often difficult world.

When Marinho and I had begun our journey, we'd both been passionate and resolute, and focused squarely on our goal. We'd been prepared to go to extremes and endure all manner of hardships – and we had.

We'd waded through filth, climbed mountains of

garbage, and scaled an abandoned skyscraper to get the footage we wanted. We'd clambered outside speeding vehicles, and walked through thousands of exploding firecrackers. We'd been threatened with murder and violence, and talked our way in and out of countless bizarre situations. We'd filmed secretly inside a refugee camp, a military base, a police internment centre, and a strip club.

Our partnership had been successful because we'd held such a firm belief in our work. When the chips were down, Marinho and I had been willing to fight harder and go further than anyone we'd yet encountered. We hadn't always been lucky, but we'd certainly been persistent.

So long as we'd been fighting together, Marinho and I had made a powerful team. When we began fighting each other, however, we very nearly tore the project apart.

Our burning hunger for justice was the only thing that made our journey possible – but once the flame turned against us, it threatened to burn down everything we'd built together.

BULLET WITH BUTTERFLY WINGS

Travelling can be hard, and any long journey can strain a relationship.

I've seen plenty of close friends and couples torn apart by life on the road. They'll break under the strain of living in each other's pockets for weeks and months at a time, while trying to negotiate unfamiliar environments with limited time, money, and knowledge.

Marinho and I had been little more than strangers when we'd begun our journey. We weren't travelling for pleasure – we were working, and it was stressful, unrewarding work. By the time we reached Vietnam, we barely had any free time. I was too busy juggling a thousand little tasks and, when Marinho wasn't working on the project, he was taking his own photographs, or working a second job from his laptop. Most of the time we were sharing the same room, because that's all we had the money for.

Marinho and I weren't just facing the usual decisions about transport, food, and accommodation. At times we were making decisions that were potentially matters of life and death for ourselves and others, and we rarely had the information we needed. The burdens we carried were immense – and, all things considered, I considered our partnership to be an incredibly successful one.

In hindsight, it's not surprising that our relationship began to unravel: it's surprising that we were able to hold it together for so long, under such intense conditions.

For a time, I felt that Marinho and I had formed a genuine friendship, which I valued. Our disagreements were rare, and passed quickly. It was admirable that there had been no major conflicts between us – but when they did finally come, they were seismic.

By April, Marinho and I were seven months into what had originally been planned as a six-month project, and the end was still nowhere in sight. We were tired, impatient, and beginning to fray.

The American meteorologist Edward Lorenz once speculated that the flapping of a butterfly's wings on one continent could trigger a tornado on another, and something very similar happened with us.

Somewhere in Europe was a man I'd never met. I didn't know his name, what he looked like, or anything else about him. Late one evening on a train, that man committed a crime that sent shockwaves through our project, and very nearly destroyed it.

Marinho and I had both made sacrifices for the sake of the project. We'd both missed Christmas and birthdays with our families, and Marinho had missed his sister's wedding. While we'd been working in Vietnam, my grandmother was dying at home in Australia, and I lost my last chance to see her again.

Marinho had an additional strain upon him: he had a girlfriend in Europe. She came to visit him while we were working in Sapa, and it wasn't hard to see why he cared so deeply about her – she was an intelligent, beautiful, vivacious woman.

Several weeks after Marinho's girlfriend returned to Europe, she was assaulted one evening when riding home on a train. It wouldn't be appropriate to share any further details here, except to say that Marinho's girlfriend had every reason to feel shaken, and Marinho had every reason to feel upset. Of course, he wished he could have been there to support his partner.

I'd never asked Marinho to sign anything. All we had was a gentleman's agreement – an informal written arrangement fleshed out by email before our journey began. Unfortunately, we hadn't allowed for these kinds of contingencies, nor did we have the resources to deal with them.

Although Marinho never raised the issue directly, he couldn't hide the fact that his heart wasn't in the project anymore. It seemed that he wanted to leave, but wouldn't let himself quit.

Marinho's behaviour became increasingly erratic.

I couldn't understand if that was part of a considered strategy, or if it was just a release for the helpless rage he felt, an outward sign of his inner turmoil.

In either case, I felt as though Marinho was trying to force me into firing him.

Marinho's situation was a terrible one, and I was truly sorry he couldn't be there for his girlfriend – but I couldn't fire him, because that would have meant the end of the project. I'd been very fortunate to find Marinho. It would be extremely difficult to replace him – and simply impossible at short notice.

I wasn't even sure that "firing" was the correct term. I didn't consider myself Marinho's boss, and ours was in no way a typical employer-employee relationship. It was a partnership: the two of us had agreed to produce the documentary together.

I'd gambled everything I had on the search for May, and – so long as I believed there was still some possibility of finding her – she came first. I intended to honour the commitments I'd made, and I could do that only if Marinho honoured his own commitments.

Perhaps there was a better solution, and we were too caught up in the moment to see it. Perhaps, like so many conflicts, it was just a matter of miscommunication.

As strange as it now seems, for all the time we spent together and all the tension between us, Marinho and I barely spoke about these things that threatened to tear us apart. We might have discussed the problem to find a solution that could work for both of us, and I'm sorry that never happened. The few words we exchanged were uttered in frustration.

Marinho's support had made an enormous difference to the project. As he began to withdraw that support and turn against the project, I struggled to understand what was happening, and I didn't want to believe it.

As Marinho began stepping back from his responsibilities, it became clear that the project would fall apart unless I stepped in to fill the void, and so I did. Only then did I realise the position I'd stepped into: by taking a firmer hand over the project, I'd become Marinho's hated figure of authority.

There is immense power in the stories we tell each other, and in the stories we tell ourselves. Until then, Marinho had seen the project as a cause worth fighting – and perhaps even dying – for. Now, it seems he began telling himself that the project was a trap in which he was caught.

Under those circumstances, it became necessary for Marinho to escape that trap, even at the cost of destroying everything we'd worked towards. Marinho began kicking harder against the project, which began spinning further and further out of control, while I struggled to restore balance.

I'd become his Goliath.

WAIT A MINUTE

On our final week in Vietnam, Marinho and I took a pair of motorbikes on a nine-hundred-kilometre roadtrip into the mountains of the far north.

From all I'd seen, the Hmong communities of northern Vietnam seemed to have a destructive approach towards the local human trafficking crisis. They seemed more focused on shaming and blaming victims rather than working to address the actual problem and the damage it caused.

My research had turned up one amazing exception: a woman named Vang Thi Mai, who lived in the northern village of Hop Tien. I'd first seen Mai's name in a 2011 article in the New York Times, and had otherwise been able to find very little information about her.

Hop Tien was in wild, remote country just a stone's throw from the Chinese border. Traffickers had been preying upon the village for more than a decade, selling its women across the border.

Some of the victims had been fortunate enough to escape China and come home – only to find themselves stigmatised, disowned by their families and outcast by their community.

Vang Thi Mai had been the chairperson of a local women's union. In 2001, she and her husband had founded a small textiles cooperative to create more jobs for local women, and to help trafficking survivors reintegrate into the community.

Risking the judgement of the other villagers, they began offering the outcast women shelter in their own home, and gave them work making bags and clothing.

The cooperative had struggled against a lack of funding and facilities, and had had trouble finding markets for its finished products. In time, however, it had become remarkably successful.

Adapting traditional designs to modern tastes, the initiative had empowered the women, boosted the local economy, and increased acceptance of trafficking survivors.

The cooperative had gradually grown to include 130 members, all Hmong, including twenty-one survivors of human trafficking and thirty survivors of domestic violence. The items they produced were now being distributed around Vietnam and the world.

I wanted to meet Mai in person, to give her a voice in our documentary. It would be a challenging journey from Sapa, but I felt it would be worth the effort.

I'd become aware of two major flaws in our documentary.

The story we were telling was about young Hmong women, and we'd given those women the most prominent role within the documentary. I wanted to give those women an international platform so that they could tell the story in their own words.

After my interview with the supposed Hmong expert had proved useless, however, the only voices of authority left in the film – Michael and Georges – were both foreign white men, as was I.

I was aware of another organisation, Pacific Links Foundation, which operated a shelter for human trafficking survivors in Lao Cai, and seemed to be managed largely by local women. I was under the impression, however, that Pacific Links was intimately connected with the Vietnamese government. As our work was necessarily hidden from the local authorities, I felt it was best to avoid Pacific Links for the time being. It would be another eight months until I was to meet any of their representatives.

If I could find Vang Thi Mai, she could share her insights into the cross-border trafficking crisis from the perspective of a local Hmong woman who had spent years challenging community norms to support survivors. Not only would Mai's be an important voice to include in the conversation, but her story could bolster our documentary in another crucial way.

Our documentary was still in desperate need of a happy ending. Regardless of how strong the story might be, if Marinho and I couldn't find a way to finish the film on a positive note, we'd struggle to find an audience for it.

My chances of finding May and Pang, and bringing them home to their families in Vietnam, were extremely slender. An interview with Vang Thi Mai seemed to be our best remaining hope for an optimistic ending.

Unfortunately, it wasn't as simple as it seemed. After riding north into the mountains, Marinho and I had trouble finding Mai, and then we had trouble speaking to her. Our usual interpreters, Chu and Chan, hadn't been able to come with us, and we couldn't find any locals who spoke English well enough to interpret for us.

Mai was a small, good-humoured woman with a round face and a gap-toothed smile. She welcomed us inside the cooperative and happily demonstrated how the hemp fibres were spun and woven into cloth. We looked over the designs and saw how they were pieced together – but the language barrier remained between us.

I took Mai's details, and she later answered my questions via email, but we never had a chance to record her story for our documentary.

Disappointed, Marinho and I decided to push on, into the northernmost extremity of Vietnam. It was a rugged and often spectacular region where shattered roads twisted around broad, stony valleys. High jagged peaks loomed on all sides, and were swallowed by the haze of distance.

The next morning, Marinho simply rode away. We hadn't yet decided on a destination for the day, and I didn't know where he was going. Nor did we have any way of contacting each other: we were in a remote region with little Internet access, and I wasn't carrying a phone.

Marinho was aware of all of those things, of course. We'd gone north to record footage for our documentary, but it seemed he'd decided to take the day off and simply disappear.

I rode all day, and didn't see Marinho again until after nightfall. I didn't know what his intentions were and I wasn't in the mood to find out. I'd learned that my grandmother had died that morning, after three days in a coma. It had been a long day and I'd had other things to think about, so I let it pass.

That episode struck me as the first in an escalating series of provocations. Marinho appeared to be testing the limits of our partnership, to see how far he could push me. By not responding, it seemed that I'd only encouraged him to more brazen acts of rebellion.

Marinho tried again almost immediately – and this time, he must have known I'd take the bait.

GENTLEMAN'S PACT

I trusted Marinho, and had been quite relaxed about our gentleman's agreement.

Marinho and I had agreed that I wouldn't be paying for his alcohol and clothing, for example – but when I realised that he wasn't a big drinker, and didn't need much clothing, I didn't mind paying for those things.

To my mind, that was only fair. Marinho had given a great deal of time and energy to our work. Though the money was tight, I was happy to make his life a little easier, especially knowing that his other job didn't pay much.

As part of our agreement, Marinho had agreed not to take any material from the project and share it anywhere else without my approval.

I didn't know if there was any real hope of bringing May or Pang home. After we'd spent all of our time, money, and energy, our stories were most likely the only thing that Marinho and I would bring back from our long and arduous journey.

Since all of the money was coming from the two fundraising campaigns or out of my own pocket, it didn't seem reasonable that Marinho could take those stories and sell them elsewhere, at least not without my consent.

Over the past seven months, Marinho had written a series of articles for a small European magazine. For some of those articles he'd asked to use material from the project. I didn't see any harm in it and had let him use whatever he wanted, asking only that the project was credited at the end of the article.

It was a simple request, and a fair one, and that arrangement had been working well for everyone involved.

Marinho had told me earlier that the magazine liked his material so much that they'd asked him to write a feature article for the next issue – it might even be the cover story.

It was exciting news, and he was thrilled. Again, he would be using material from the project, and I was happy for him to do so.

Before we returned to Sapa from the northern mountains, Marinho casually mentioned that the project would not be credited on his feature article. It wasn't presented as a question, or a matter for discussion: it was stated as a hard fact.

After seven months living together, sharing countless bus rides, meals, and hotel rooms, Marinho and I had become like an old married couple. We knew each other's habits and values. We knew what was acceptable, and what was not, within the context of our relationship. We knew how the pieces fit together, and we knew when something was out of place.

There was no doubt that Marinho's statement was a challenge. He'd left me only two choices: I could ignore him, and let him trample on the agreement we'd made, or I could draw a line in the sand.

I was concerned by the idea of Marinho taking our material and sharing it without any acknowledgement. Marinho had access to seven months' worth of material – if I didn't say something this time, perhaps he wouldn't even tell me next time. He hadn't signed anything; I couldn't stop him.

What Marinho really wanted, though, was not to share our stories without my consent – he wanted to go home to his girlfriend. He wanted the project to end, but he didn't want to be the one to finish it.

I had no doubt that Marinho's remark was intended to incite conflict between us. Perhaps he was hoping to damage the project enough that he could slip out through the cracks and go home.

I could understand Marinho's position, but it stood in direct opposition to my own.

The project had been born from my determination to do everything I could to find and help May, and a stubborn refusal to back down for anyone. I'd assumed that any opposition I'd meet would come from traffickers and their accomplices, the criminal and the corrupt. I'd assumed it would be a black and white situation, with the villains on one side and their victims on the other. Never had I imagined it would become so morally complex.

I was certain that this would be my only chance to help May and Pang. When Marinho and I finished our journey, the only money still remaining would be the funds we'd already committed to finishing our documentary. I couldn't keep fundraising for the same search when the only result had been failure and defeat, and I had no more money of my own – I'd long since spent all of my savings on the project.

To hold the project together and have any hope of finding May, I'd have to take a hard line against someone I'd considered a friend. I didn't feel good about it, but I didn't see any other option.

If I didn't stand up for myself and the project this time, I was certain that Marinho would keep pushing me until I did – and the longer I let his behaviour continue, the harder it would be to stop. It was a precarious situation that could easily spiral out of control.

I didn't react to Marinho's challenge immediately, however: I understood the need for caution. I'd have to remind Marinho of his responsibilities under the agreement we'd made, and I'd have to be firm – but I'd also have to be very careful not to create any conflict between us, which he might use as an excuse to end the project.

I decided to wait a little, to consider my options and respond when the time was right. Unfortunately, it didn't quite happen that way.

Our final stop in Vietnam was to be Hanoi. Marinho left Sapa one day ahead of me, to have some broken equipment repaired. I stayed behind to record some extra material for the documentary.

I wasn't sure what to say to Marinho. I knew that the future of the project depended on this conversation, so I didn't want to rush in and bungle it.

In the end, though, I just couldn't contain myself any longer. I've never been good at pretending that things are fine when they're not, and I have a habit of blurting out my true thoughts and feelings at inappropriate moments.

Before I left Sapa, I sent Marinho a message saying I wasn't comfortable for the magazine to publish any of our material without acknowledgement.

Marinho responded immediately.

"Those stories don't belong to anyone," he told me. Maybe the magazine would mention the project and maybe it wouldn't, he said, but they had no responsibility towards me.

"It's not their responsibility I'm thinking of, it's yours," I told him.

"I don't have any responsibility," he replied.

I didn't know what Marinho had used in his article

– he didn't want to show it to me. He told me I could see it when it was printed, like everyone else.

I barely slept on the night bus back to Hanoi, and by the time it rolled into the capital at dawn, I was exhausted. My frustration with Marinho had been building like a slow fire inside me, and I didn't have the patience to contain it anymore. The project was already draining enough of my energy without Marinho adding any complications of his own.

Marinho was waiting for me at a guesthouse in Hanoi's old quarter. It was our last full day in Vietnam, and it very nearly became the last day of the project.

Before I met Marinho at the guesthouse, we'd already sent a series of messages back and forth, and the situation had begun spiralling out of control.

"I want to raise awareness of human trafficking, and I'm happy to see you publishing articles to do so," I told him. "But if you're using our material, it requires appropriate acknowledgement."

"No," he said. "End of story".

Marinho told me I didn't understand the law. I said I wasn't talking about legalities, I was talking about morality.

"I'm not going to discuss this with you anymore," he said. "I want this project to be finished as soon as possible."

At last, we'd reached the heart of the matter.

May was "impossible to reach", Marinho told me. We'd already spent three months trying to find her, and that was more than enough.

It was time to call off the search for May, he said – he was no longer willing to be part of it.

The project was rapidly unravelling, and I didn't know how to hold it together.

MAN IN BLACK

Since my first meeting with Michael in January, I'd been hoping to arrange an interview with X.

X was as close as anyone could get to human trafficking without actually being a victim or a trafficker. The more I learned about this horrendous industry, the more I came to appreciate his phenomenal courage, sacrifice, and moral strength.

X had been physically rescuing trafficking victims for years. He regularly ventured alone into life-threatening situations, and returned home with girls who otherwise had no hope of escaping by themselves.

X had rescued Vu, and had gone to China in the hopes of rescuing Pang. If we ever succeeded in locating May, he would be the person we'd call on to help bring her home. X was a major part of the story we'd be telling in our documentary, and a well-recorded interview with him could make a huge difference in helping people understand the realities of human trafficking.

I'd wanted to meet (and, if possible, interview) X since I'd first learned of his existence, but he proved to be an exceptionally difficult man to catch. After three months, I still hadn't even had a chance to speak with X personally, and every attempt to meet him had fallen through.

X was a very busy man, and his schedule was highly unpredictable. He travelled frequently, often at extremely short notice, and it was very difficult to know when he might be in the office.

Michael had handled all of our communication. We'd bounced countless messages back and forth as we struggled to arrange a time.

At last – after three months – Michael and I were able to pin down a time when it seemed that Michael, X, Marinho, and I would all be available: on our very last afternoon in Vietnam. It was our final chance – if this meeting fell through, there wouldn't be another.

Four days before the meeting, Michael said something had come up and he wouldn't be able to make it – but X "should be there".

X was interested to meet me and share information, but he had very little time available. He could give us a maximum of twenty minutes, and hoped we'd be able to finish in fifteen.

He'd been reluctant to agree to a formal interview at all. While he'd now given his consent, it would have to be handled carefully. Blue Dragon was trying to keep X out of the public eye, and we couldn't show his face.

I'd submitted a list of questions I wanted to ask X. I was told that he wouldn't be comfortable speaking about his personal life or motivations, any government issues, or any details about the rescues.

It would be our most challenging interview, but it would also be one of our most important. I knew it was an incredible opportunity and I wanted to make the most of it.

When I arrived at the guesthouse, the atmosphere was tense between Marinho and myself – but we were professionals, and we had a job to do. It was going to be a big day for us. I showered, changed, and revised my list of questions.

I'd half-expected X to be called away for other work, forcing us to cancel the interview, but Blue Dragon hadn't said anything. It seemed as though everything would be going ahead according to schedule. I crossed my fingers.

Marinho and I had agreed to leave the guesthouse at half-past twelve, and the time came. Marinho hadn't appeared yet. I was about to go in search of him when he stepped into the room.

Marinho said he wasn't coming to the interview – to teach me a lesson, he later told me. He turned around, walked out of the guesthouse, and disappeared into the alleyway outside.

KEEP MY COMPOSURE

Marinho had sabotaged one of our most important interviews.

He'd timed his announcement deliberately, waiting for the moment when he knew its impact would be the most devastating.

I was furious, but there was nothing I could do: I had to get to Blue Dragon to meet with X.

I'd been working on the assumption that Marinho and his equipment would be present for the interview. I lost a few precious minutes struggling to gather my manic thoughts and double-checking I had everything I'd need to record the interview myself, then I rushed out as quickly as I could.

I arrived at Blue Dragon hot, flustered, and late. X was available only for a twenty-minute window, and that time was already slipping past.

I cursed Marinho under my breath. I wasn't going to forget this, or simply let it pass. I didn't know what would happen when I saw him again, but I was sure it wasn't going to be pretty.

In the meantime, I had an interview to record.

Blue Dragon's communications manager led me upstairs to where X was waiting. It was an honour to finally meet him in person.

I can't tell you what X looked like – except to say that he didn't fit the popular, macho image of a hero. His work relied on intelligence, rather than brute strength. He was quiet, dignified, and polite: more a Clark Kent than a Superman.

It was a hurried, botched interview, as I worked to guide the conversation while also monitoring the equipment. The microphones were set up hastily, and we barely touched the list of questions I'd wanted to ask – there just wasn't time.

In Sapa, I'd conducted long, meandering interviews to conceal my true purpose. This was just the opposite: I cut straight to the chase.

It seemed that Blue Dragon's own investigations had stalled. X had also tried, and failed, to get May's "real" Chinese phone number from her family.

He'd been receiving assistance from a friend in Sapa, he said. His friend had also met with May's family, but they hadn't been very cooperative and had volunteered very little information.

May's family had given the friend a number which

they'd claimed to be May's Chinese phone number – but when X had tried to call it, it didn't work. It looked like a Chinese number, he said, but it wasn't. Without a contact number for May, there was nothing X could do for her.

I realised that the friend X was referring to was, in fact, Vu. I knew that Vu had also been asking around for May's second Chinese number, and she'd seemed to have more than a casual interest in it.

X told me that Vu had been speaking with Pang in the Hmong language on his behalf. Blue Dragon had given Vu her freedom – it was not surprising that she would want to help them with other cases, especially when the girls they were working to find were her own friends.

There were times I'd felt Vu had been acting somewhat erratically, and hadn't been telling me everything. I hadn't been sure quite what to make of it – but when I realised she'd been working secretly with Blue Dragon, any doubts I might have had were laid to rest.

I found it amusing that Vu and I had both been digging around in the same small patch of dirt in search of the exact same things, without sharing the full extent of our work with each other. No doubt Blue Dragon had cautioned Vu to secrecy, just as they had me, and it seemed she'd done a better job than I had.

I asked X about Pang's situation. He'd spoken to her four or five times, but said he'd had trouble communicating with her. Pang didn't seem able to speak

Vietnamese, Chinese, or English very well. It seemed she'd even begun to forget her own mother tongue, the Hmong language, so it had been impossible for X to find out where she was.

There had been another tragic complication, too. In late February or early March – when I'd been in the middle of my own investigation, and X had been struggling to find Pang in China – Pang's youngest child had succumbed to illness and died. Pang had been struck by grief, which had only made it more difficult for X to pinpoint her location.

This detail helped explain some of the confusion over the number of children Pang had in China, although it still wasn't clear whether she had one or two surviving children.

I'd arrived in Asia with the assumption that, if we did ever succeed in finding May or Pang, then the rest would be simple. Blue Dragon would organise their rescues and bring them home.

I'd since come to realise, however, that May and Pang's circumstances had become incredibly complicated. Because they now had children in China, they would both essentially be forced to choose between their children and their own freedom.

Even if we could find May and Pang, they might not want to come home.

It wasn't a matter of simply finding and rescuing the girls, but of giving them the time they needed to solve their dilemmas in their own way. May and Pang would have to find the solution they felt was best for themselves, for their families, and for their children. It was our role to respect their decisions, and to offer any assistance they might require.

There was one crucial difference between May and Pang's situations, however. X said it was clear that Pang's family wanted her to come home – but he didn't see the same desire in May's family. While neither of us could understand the attitude May's family had taken, it would only make May's decision even more difficult for her.

X and I spoke briefly about the girls he'd rescued from Chinese brothels, and then our time was up. He had other matters demanding his attention, and I thanked him for his time.

What could have – and should have – been a major interview for our documentary had been a shambles. I didn't know if I'd be able to salvage anything from it for the film, but X had given me plenty to think about. As I stepped back out into the afternoon glare, I began to put the pieces together, and realised that there still might be a chance for me to help May.

But first, I'd have to deal with Marinho.

ALL FIRED UP

I was livid with Marinho. It was tempting to go directly back to the guesthouse and tell him exactly how I felt about him – but if I wanted to continue my search for May, I'd have to make peace with him, and win him over.

It wasn't going to be easy to bring him back to the project, just as he was tearing loose. I'd have to play my cards very calmly, and very carefully. I couldn't risk another repeat of what had happened that morning: that would certainly mean the end of my search.

I took a long walk through the city to calm myself down. The interview had been at one o'clock, and night had fallen by the time I arrived back at the guesthouse. I was surprised to find Marinho standing outside in the darkness of the alleyway, waiting for me.

He had something in his hand: I couldn't see what it

was. As I approached, he raised it almost to eye level and shoved it towards me, cursing me in his native tongue. I was familiar with the term he used: it could be translated as "piece of shit".

The object in his hand was a 32Gb memory card he'd taken from his camera. With everything else that had happened that day, I didn't stop to wonder what the significance of the memory card might have been. I took it, slipped it into my wallet, and didn't think about it until afterwards. For the moment, I had other things to worry about.

Marinho was enraged with me, though not for any reason I might have guessed. It had nothing to do with our argument that morning – it was because I hadn't fed him yet.

As part of our agreement, I was providing all of Marinho's food and accommodation while he was working on the project. I usually gave him money for expenses, but it seemed he'd already spent it all. As it was our final day in Vietnam, he hadn't wanted to withdraw any money of his own, so he hadn't eaten any dinner.

I hadn't known what to expect on my return to the guesthouse, and had mentally prepared myself for all sorts of possibilities – but this was just too strange and illogical. Was he so desperate to start a fight that he was prepared to use any excuse, even the most absurd?

I wondered how long he'd been standing out in the alleyway, stewing in his own juices. Why had he chosen to confront me there, rather than simply waiting inside?

It was true that I hadn't fed him. I hadn't done it deliberately; I hadn't realised he was out of money, and – with everything else that was happening – hadn't even thought about it.

Had I breached our agreement? I didn't know. Did we even still have an agreement? Was Marinho even still part of the project? I wasn't sure about that, either. He certainly wasn't acting like it.

It seemed Marinho had wanted me to fire him – and there were several times that afternoon when I'd considered that possibility. It seemed bizarre that he should now suddenly be so concerned with the agreement he'd completely disregarded all day.

Ours had originally been conceived as a six-month journey, though we'd both acknowledged from the beginning that we were flexible and willing to accommodate the demands of the project. As the investigation had proved worth pursuing, Marinho and I had discussed and agreed upon extensions to the original six-month period.

Earlier that day, Marinho had told me those extensions were meaningless and he would no longer honour them, because they hadn't been made in writing. That seemed to make a difference to him – that a commitment had to be written down to be considered valid. At the same time, though, he'd also tossed aside the written commitments he'd made to myself and the project.

I realised it was foolish to try to understand Marinho's underlying logic: at that moment, he seemed to be acting on pure emotion.

How could I reason with a man like that? How could I appeal to the logic of someone who had already abandoned it? What sense was there in a man who had deliberately shattered his own agreements, and was now raging at me for inadvertently slipping up on one of mine?

Marinho didn't seem to have any grasp of the fact that my infraction had come on the heels of a much more serious offence of his own. He'd deliberately sabotaged our interview with X to teach me a lesson, and told me so. It had been done in cold blood, in a way that had been calculated to cause the most damage to the project and leave me in the worst possible situation. Now he seemed righteous about it, perhaps even proud of what he'd done, while he raved at me for not having bought him dinner.

There was no point highlighting Marinho's contradictory behaviour; that wouldn't help me now. There was no sense fuming over the things that had happened earlier that day, and how much better the interview might have been handled. Unless I could defuse the situation and find a way to bring Marinho back on side, my search for May was already over.

THE MASTERPLAN

There was a little place nearby that sold bowls of noodle soup, and we went inside. Marinho ordered food while I tried to understand the situation.

It seemed that Marinho planned to continue with the project – or, at least, some of it.

Our Vietnamese visas were expiring the next day, and we were going to China: we both seemed to agree on that much. The question was, what would we be doing in China?

Marinho felt that the search for May was a waste of time, and he didn't want anything more to do with it. He wanted to scratch May from our list, and finish searching for the other 99 people. While we'd still have twenty-seven people to search for, they were concentrated in just six locations: three in China, two in Nepal, and only one in India.

Marinho wanted to do only what was necessary to finish the project, and do it as quickly as possible, then he wanted to go home. The journey itself would be an incredibly long one, taking us fifteen thousand kilometres by road and rail – but if we pushed ourselves, it could all be done in a matter of weeks.

After everything that had happened that day, there was a part of me that would have been happy to be rid of Marinho, but I wasn't yet ready to give up on the search for May. So long as there was any chance of finding her, I was determined to take it.

I had to convince Marinho that there was still some hope. I told him what I'd learned that afternoon at Blue Dragon, and explained my plan.

X had told me that Pang had her own phone in China, and had been given the freedom to make and receive phonecalls at any time. Although he thought that Pang's "husband" might be concerned if he heard Pang speaking English on the phone, X felt it was probably safe for me to call her. I was advised to tread carefully.

I wanted to go to China, to contact Pang, and to try to find her. Blue Dragon had offered to rescue Pang, if that's what she wanted – but they couldn't rescue her until they had her exact location, and they'd had trouble communicating with her. Blue Dragon was juggling a lot of cases with limited resources, and they didn't have as much time to focus on Pang's case.

Pang was a friend of mine. When I'd first been living in Sapa, we'd been able to understand each other in

English, and I was confident we could do so again. Blue Dragon believed that Pang was somewhere in Guangdong province, in southeast China. If I could determine her precise location, I could pass that information back to Blue Dragon, and they could then rescue her at any time she chose.

But there was another reason I wanted to speak to Pang: she was the only remaining person who could give me May's second Chinese phone number.

May's father had made it clear he would never give me the number, and he wouldn't allow anyone else from his family to give it to me. Zao might have the number, but she refused to speak to me. Pang's mother didn't have it anymore – but Pang had it, and I was sure that she would give it to me.

If I could call Pang, then I should be able to call May – and then we'd have a very real chance of finding her.

I really didn't know how much time I might need to contact the girls and determine their locations: it would be a complex undertaking, and there were still so many unknown factors.

The real question was, how much time would Marinho be prepared to give me?

A month would be ideal, but I knew he'd never agree to that. I doubted he'd even give me two weeks, and I was sure it would be impossible to do it in much less than that.

Give me ten days, I said.

In any case, our first stop would be Yangshuo, a

Chinese city seven hundred kilometres northeast of Hanoi. In Yangshuo, we'd be searching for one of the 99 people I'd previously photographed. We'd then have to decide whether to turn right or left, east or west.

East would take us to Guangdong province, to search for Pang. West would take us across the Tibetan plateau into Nepal and India, to the end of our journey.

From Yangshuo, I could try calling Pang. If I got through, and could communicate with her, we would already be halfway to Guangdong to search for her. With any luck, we would also succeed in contacting May, and could turn north to begin narrowing down her location.

Marinho was behaving more reasonably now that he had food in his stomach. He considered what I'd told him, and seemed to agree there was still some hope of finding May. He said he'd give me ten days, but that was all.

I'd brokered a fragile truce between us, but I didn't know if it would last – and now the clock was ticking.

SABOTAGE

As long and exhausting as it had been, our final day in Vietnam still held one more surprise.

Three days earlier, before we'd left Sapa, Marinho and I had filmed one last interview there.

Vu's aunt Big Zao had invited us to her home, in one of the villages outside town. There, over the course of a forty-five minute interview, she had shared her experiences of being tricked and trafficked into China. Big Zao recounted her daring escape and return home (while six months' pregnant to her Chinese "husband"), and told us of her life since then.

It was an inspirational story, and a fascinating interview. As she spoke, Big Zao's half-Chinese son lay in her lap. Now four and a half years old, he was a good-looking boy with large dark eyes and close-cropped hair.

As usual, I'd conducted the interview while Marinho

had operated both cameras. My camera had been set up to capture a very simple, fixed angle of Big Zao's head and shoulders, leaving Marinho to capture a more varied and carefully-monitored mixture of shots with his own camera.

I later discovered that my camera had been set up incorrectly: the entire interview was overexposed, and would be unusable for our documentary. I assumed that was accidental, rather than anything malicious on Marinho's part. In any case, the only reliable footage that remained of the interview had been captured on Marinho's camera.

After each interview, I'd copy the video files to an external hard drive I carried. That hard drive contained the growing accumulation of footage from which Marinho and I planned to construct our documentary. The hard drive increased in value with every passing day, and with each new file copied to it.

I hadn't yet had a chance to back up Marinho's footage of Big Zao's interview. In fact, with everything else that had been happening, I'd forgotten all about it.

After brokering our fragile truce that evening, Marinho and I returned to the guesthouse. He remained downstairs in the lobby, while I went up to our room. It had been a long, strange day, and I took a moment to sit down and collect my thoughts.

As I reflected on the events of the past few hours, I remembered the 32Gb memory card Marinho had handed me in the alleyway outside the hotel. I realised it was the memory card from his camera, containing the only reliable footage of our interview with Big Zao.

I took the card out of my wallet and loaded it into my laptop. It was empty. I was confused, and messaged Marinho downstairs: "There's nothing on this card...?"

Marinho assured me that the interview with Big Zao was there. I checked the card again using first my camera and then an external card reader. There was nothing.

"I'm sure it's not empty," he told me – but it was. I asked Marinho to check his other cards.

"I'm one hundred percent sure everything was on the 32Gb," he said.

Over the past seven months, Marinho and I had had more than our share of problems with data and equipment. Near the beginning of our journey, in Indonesia, another memory card had failed in the worst possible way. Not only had the contents disappeared completely, but our laptops and cameras had stopped recognising the card at all. I hadn't been able to recover the data, or even reformat the card. There was no obvious reason for the error: it seemed to have happened spontaneously.

But this was different. There didn't seem to be any error with the card itself. It functioned perfectly in the laptop, camera, and external card reader. The interview had simply vanished.

Perhaps I could still recover the data, I didn't know. I couldn't even think about that yet: there were too many other things happening in my head.

I remembered Marinho's fury at my late return, and the odd way he'd been standing in the alleyway, waiting for me. I remembered how he'd thrust the card towards me and cursed me.

It had been three days since our interview and, with all the dramas of the past twenty-four hours, that card had been the last thing on my mind. Why had Marinho chosen that particular moment to hand it to me?

He must have handed me memory cards a hundred times over the past seven months, but never so dramatically, and never with a curse.

My mind clouded with suspicion, and I no longer knew what to believe.

Was Marinho innocent, and telling me the truth? Was it just a freak occurrence that the data had disappeared on that day, of all days? That he'd just happened to hand me the card at that moment, of all moments?

Or was Marinho guilty, and compounding his guilt with lies? While I'd been rushing across the city to interview X, had Marinho been sitting there at the guesthouse, deleting our footage? Had he been waiting outside for me in the alley because he'd wanted to distance himself from the scene of his crime?

Marinho had been brought to Asia to do a job. Not only had he failed to do that job, but – at a critical moment, when he knew there would be no second chances – he'd deliberately sabotaged the job, making it as difficult as possible for me to do it.

He'd done it to teach me a lesson, he'd said, though

it still wasn't clear what that lesson was supposed to be.

Not only had Marinho sabotaged our present work and cast the future of the project into uncertainty, it now seemed he'd gone one step further and had begun destroying our past. I had no proof of his new treachery, but the circumstantial evidence seemed clear enough.

Worst of all, Marinho's tactics had worked. He knew that I needed him to continue the project. In desperation, I'd rewarded his treachery with more power, and he'd used that power to draw limits around the project.

The next day, Marinho and I would be leaving Hanoi and crossing into China, where we'd be facing potentially life-threatening situations together. We'd be cut off from all immediate support but each other, and it was critical that there was trust between us.

Trust is the foundation of every human relationship. Until recently, I would have trusted Marinho with my life. Now, I didn't know if I could trust him at all.

How far was Marinho willing to go? What would he destroy or damage next time he wanted more power, or wanted to teach me another "lesson"?

I looked down at the external hard drive sitting beside my laptop. That hard drive contained all the fruits of our labours from the past seven months. It held dozens of interviews, including those with Michael, Georges, and X, as well as with May and Pang's friends and families. It had all of the footage Marinho and I had collected in Sapa and the northern mountains over the past three and a half months. That's where we kept the abduction

Marinho had captured, and our copy of Vu's wedding DVD.

Many of those things were irreplaceable.

I could hardly believe that Marinho might want to destroy any of the footage we'd worked so hard to collect, but I could hardly believe the other things he'd done that day, either.

I had to keep the drive safe – but Marinho and I were working on the documentary together, and denying him access to it now would only cause more conflict between us. The last thing we needed was more conflict.

I was almost certain that Marinho had deleted Big Zao's interview – but even if I'd had the proof, I couldn't accuse him of the crime. I still needed him, if I was to have any hope of finding May.

Very soon, I would find out whether all of my efforts had been worthwhile and I had a real chance of meeting May and Pang – or if the entire project had just been a colossal waste of time and energy.

As the immediate tension of my conflict with Marinho began to ease, I reflected on the magnitude of the task I'd set myself, and examined the ten-day deadline with clearer eyes.

Somewhere out there in the immensity of China, May and Pang were waiting. How could I ever hope to find them both in just ten days? I'd have to cover vast distances, and decipher any clues I was able to obtain along the way. Even if I already had May and Pang's exact locations, it would take half of those ten days just to reach them both.

Perhap Marinho had known, from the moment I'd suggested it, that I'd set myself an impossible task. Perhaps he'd only agreed to give me ten more days so that he could say he'd given me a chance. Perhaps he and I weren't so different after all, and this search was my Goliath.

I'd bought myself a little time – but at what price, and what was it worth? What could I realistically hope to do with ten days? All I'd gained was a tentative peace with Marinho which hadn't really solved anything, and was already crumbling around me.

I'd been told that the First World War had left so many tensions and unresolved issues that the Second World War had become unavoidable. I didn't know much about that. I did know that a second conflict with Marinho was now inevitable, and it was certain to be bigger and uglier than the first.

There was bad blood between us now. Marinho and I had begun pulling the project in different directions – and, across the border in China, we would finally tear it apart.

It was only a matter of time, and the countdown had begun.

Michael had emphasised the need to proceed slowly and carefully, to take the time to consider all possibilities in advance. I'd seen for myself how dangerous it could be to ignore that advice – but now I didn't seem to have any other option. If I was to have any hope at all of finding May and Pang, I'd have to race full-throttle into situations that could endanger all of our lives.

I'd promised myself I would do whatever I could to help May and Pang – but what if that involved jeopardising their safety, and risking their lives?

The decisions I would soon be forced to make in China were, morally and emotionally, some of the most difficult I have ever made. Within days, for the first time in almost four years, I would be speaking with both May and Pang – but how far would I have to go to find them?

A MESSAGE FROM
GEORGES BLANCHARD

Founder of Alliance Anti-Trafic

Human trafficking between Vietnam and China is not a new phenomenon.

In the library of Macau, we've uncovered documents which are three hundred years old describing the trafficking of Vietnamese people by the Chinese.

A century ago, André Baudrit wrote 'Bétail humain' ('Human livestock') about the abduction and sale of women and children for sex and labour in the region.

Now, in the twenty-first century, it is believed that the human trafficking issue is more terrible than ever and continues to grow with each passing year. Only in recent decades have we begun to formulate a coordinated response towards the crisis.

The United Nations hadn't even developed a

definition of human trafficking until the year 2000, and their Trafficking in Persons Protocol didn't come into effect until the final week of 2003.

It wasn't until that same year that the Vietnamese government finally, formally acknowledged the issue of human trafficking, and began to recognise victims as victims rather than criminals.

In 1995, I was operating a school for street children in Ho Chi Minh City, when two of my students – both eight-year-old girls – were kidnapped. By chance, the Vietnamese police recovered the girls at the Cambodian border.

This was my first involvement with the world of human trafficking. At that time, there were few NGOs working against human trafficking, and none in Vietnam. I saw the need for a cross-border alliance, and began to network with organisations in Cambodia and Thailand.

By 2002, we'd developed a regional taskforce involving six countries, and in 2004, we performed the first-ever rescue and repatriation of victims trafficked for sex slavery to Malaysia, Singapore, Thailand, and Laos.

Today, in 2020, Alliance Anti-Trafic is part of a group coordinated by Interpol, involving organisations in 35 countries. We've rescued or supported 8,330 Southeast Asian victims, including 5,580 from Vietnam. We've repatriated victims from 22 countries, and have assisted almost 70,000 women and teenagers involved in prostitution.

Our work is not easy, and is constantly changing. The human trafficking networks have great advantages over us.

As has been pointed out by the Thai lawyer Khun Sampasit, when traffickers need to change strategies they can do so immediately, and without budgetary concerns. Anti-trafficking groups, on the other hand, need a minimum of two years to justify their projects and wait for funding. By the time they're able to act, the situation has already changed.

Traffickers are constantly changing their methodologies and, no matter what we might do, our projects quickly become obsolete. All the reports and research on human trafficking face the same problem, forcing us to continually re-evaluate our targets.

The trafficking networks have another powerful advantage over us: it is part of human nature to fall prey to greed and temptation. It is very easy for the authorities deployed against human trafficking to become corrupted by the traffickers, especially in impoverished regions.

It's not easy to do our work when many of the figures of authority who are supposedly helping us are actually working against us. Without their complicity, I'm sure that the magnitude of the problem would be far smaller than it is now.

Alliance Anti-Trafic is now involved in the Asia Region Law Enforcement Management Program (ARLEMP), a joint initiative by the Australian Federal Police and the Royal Melbourne Institute of Technology, which aims to strengthen the response of regional law enforcement to organised crime.

One of the best weapons we have in the fight against human trafficking is education. By helping at-risk communities understand the dangers that threaten them, we help them build individual and community protection.

Alliance Anti-Trafic developed our first 'Watch Dogs' groups amongst communities in Thailand fifteen years ago. These help us identify potential victims before they become victims.

Unfortunately, we haven't been able to run the same program here in Vietnam. Vietnam is a particularly complicated country for NGOs to operate in, and the political structure here makes it extremely difficult to develop certain projects.

In response, many organisations simply turn away from Vietnam, preferring to focus on countries that are easier to work in.

Personally, I don't believe that's a good solution. These kinds of challenges should make us only more determined to help, and to allocate resources where they are most needed.

It's incredibly difficult to succeed in the fight against human trafficking, but that's what we need to do, and to keep doing. If we can't help the people who need it most, regardless of the obstacles we face, then we ourselves begin to lose our humanity.

A SPECIAL PREVIEW OF

THE MAN'S MACHINE

PART THREE OF THE INCREDIBLE
TRUE STORY BEHIND THE ACCLAIMED
'SISTERS FOR SALE' DOCUMENTARY

GOING UNDERGROUND

I first began exploring caves as a teenager.

A cave is a dark and alien world which exists beneath our own, hidden just beyond the reach of the light.

There's a thrill of primal terror in caves. It grows from the darkness, the silence, the sense of being utterly isolated from the world, not knowing what might lie in wait around the next corner.

Often, the only danger comes from your own imagination – when a sudden storm of bats erupts from the gloom, or when you find yourself nose-to-nose with a spider in a tight space. You stumble across the skeletons of creatures that once tumbled down shafts from the world above, or sought shelter and became lost in inky labyrinths, and you envisage yourself in similar situations.

There are times, however, when the dangers are real.

Failing lights. Rockslides. Poisonous gases. Flash floods. Losing your way, or losing your nerve. Setting ropes with numb and tired fingers. Skirting the slippery edges of long drops into nothingness.

It can be difficult, sometimes, to tell the true dangers from the imagined ones.

Every cave holds a treasure, and it's one of the most valuable treasures of all: self-discovery. There, in a blackness and silence more profound than you could ever find in the world above, you truly come to know yourself.

How far will you go before you turn back? What risks are you willing to take, what hardships will you endure? When you're alone in that claustrophobic darkness far beyond your comfort zone, cut off from everything you know and love, what kind of creature do you become?

Exploring an unknown cave without a map is caving at its most unpredictable. You might find yourself in giant, three-dimensional puzzles, where monolithic slabs tilt at dizzying angles. You might leap from one shelf to the next, with the black void yawning below. You might wade through icy pools, or squirm along on your belly with the whole world pushing down from above.

All you can do is to keep driving forward, by any means possible. You feel your way through, scouring the cracks and crevices for any available opening. At any moment, the passage might twist away in strange new directions, narrow down to become impassable, or open suddenly to vast, unimagined chambers.

If you're lucky, the cave might let you through to daylight. More often, though, you'll be forced to turn back, no matter how tenacious you might be. The way ahead might be blocked by stone, water, or noxious gases. Sometimes you won't have the necessary skills or equipment to continue – and sometimes the limit you reach will be your own. Sometimes the darkness wins, and you just can't find the strength you need to push forward.

When Marinho and I entered China in April 2014, we didn't enter the China of pandas and terracotta warriors, of the Great Wall and the Forbidden City. We weren't going to any of the places travellers typically went. Nor were we entering the world of apartments, factories, farms, schools, and offices that formed the daily reality for China's thirteen hundred million inhabitants.

Marinho and I were going underground, into the black world of human trafficking.

In China, as in every other country around the globe, very few people are conscious of the vast criminal underworld that exists in parallel with the world they know. Most of it is hidden just out of sight, and those who glimpse it rarely understand what they're seeing.

Few people understand that the foundations of their world are rotten with dark and secret passageways. That tens of millions of human beings like themselves are being shoved through networks of shadowy tunnels towards brutal lives in brothels, sweatshops, and other people's homes.

In that darkness, there are countless hidden places teeming with voiceless, vulnerable people who can't find their way back to the world above. Some of those people have been taken forcibly below, many were lured there, and others simply slipped through the cracks.

In 2010, I'd been living in Sapa, a small town nestled amongst the misty mountains of northern Vietnam. That's where I'd met May and Pang, two teenage girls of the local Hmong minority.

May and Pang had spent their days on the streets selling embroidered handicrafts. They took tourists trekking to nearby villages, where the girls' own families lived in poverty.

The following year, in separate incidents, May and Pang had been kidnapped from Sapa and carried off into that terrifying world of human trafficking. Each girl had been spirited across the border and forced into marriage with a stranger in some distant part of China.

The girls were still there somewhere, hidden away in that shadow world. It had been years since any of their friends or family had seen them.

Blue Dragon Children's Foundation – a Hanoi-based organisation which rescues Vietnamese girls from China – had investigated May and Pang's disappearances, but their search had stalled due to a lack of concrete information.

May and Pang's own deeply patriarchal community was doing little to fight the human trafficking crisis that had erupted in its midst, more often choosing to shame and blame its victims.

With no one else willing or able to find them, I'd returned to Asia to see if there was anything I could do to help my friends – but I'd never expected things to progress so far so quickly. I'd initially seen my role as that of a storyteller, someone who was gathering and sharing information about May and Pang's abductions to help other girls at risk of being trafficked. In recent months, I'd found myself being drawn ever-deeper into their story – and now, on entering China, I was stepping directly onto the stage.

There are many people – particularly men, it seems – who feel the need to prove themselves against the world. I was not one of them. This wasn't a part I'd ever wanted or expected to play: I had zero interest in living out any macho hero fantasies, or twisting May and Pang's story into some kind of white saviour narrative. I just wanted to help my friends, whatever that might take.

I felt a greatly increased weight of responsibility upon me. May and Pang were in precarious situations, and the decisions I made now would have direct, lasting, and potentially very serious impacts – not only on their own lives, but on entire families in both Vietnam and China. To make matters worse, I would be making those decisions largely in the dark, with insufficient time, money, or information.

It was a time of paranoia and claustrophobia, marked by doubt and second-guessing. When things happened they happened suddenly, seismically, and changed the landscape completely: the ceiling would cave in, or a chasm would open beneath my feet, and I'd be forced to find a new path forward.

You should never go below ground alone or unprepared. You need equipment you can depend on, and a partner you can trust with your life.

I'd returned to Asia with Marinho, a European cameraperson who was filming my investigation. Together, we were producing a documentary to raise awareness of the local human trafficking crisis.

In Vietnam, I'd met startling resistance from three of the people I'd expected to be most supportive of my work. May's own father Lung had done all he could to thwart me, May's best friend Zao had refused even to speak to me, and – on our very last day in Vietnam – Marinho himself had sabotaged our work.

It had been a devastating betrayal, and a shock I was still struggling to process. I'd left Vietnam defeated – and yet there was still hope.

In recent months, for the first time since they'd been kidnapped three years earlier, both May and Pang had made contact from China. Though I hadn't yet called it, I now had Pang's Chinese number, and it seemed that Pang had May's number.

I wanted to follow my friends down into that vast, shadowy world of human trafficking, to do whatever I could to help them. Contacting the girls should be simple enough, I thought – the real challenge would be finding them.

May and Pang had been swallowed up by the immense geography of a country that was larger than the United States, including Alaska, and held four times as many people.

Was there any real hope of reaching them? I wouldn't know until I'd explored all possibilities, and discovered where the limits lay: both the limits of my investigation, and of myself. How deep was I willing to venture into that darkness?

Marinho and I were travelling light, on a tight budget. We carried only the most basic equipment, and much of it had been damaged or destroyed before we'd even entered China – but that was the least of our problems. Our partnership was rapidly disintegrating, and there was no longer any trust between us. Marinho wanted to end the project and go home, while I was determined to do whatever I could to help May and Pang.

Now the two of us were stepping into darkness. We didn't know what we might find there, or how it might test us. In China, we would face threats both real and imagined. We'd be surrounded by danger on all sides – and now I felt as though I had a knife at my back.

If I was to have any chance of finding May and Pang, I'd have to get past Marinho first.

Order 'The Man's Machine' now
and make a difference at
www.sistersforsale.com

ACKNOWLEDGEMENTS

This was a challenging investigation, and a complex book to assemble. Thanks to everyone who made it possible, especially my family.

A very special thank you to Chan, Chu, and Marinho, without whom the investigation would have been impossible; to Judith Cooper, Dr. Michelle Imison, and Brittnay Mayhue for their revisions and corrections; and to Georges Blanchard for his excellent contribution.

Thanks also to Debbie Lee and Justine Bylo for their support and encouragement, Rachael McDiarmid for her promotional talents, and 'The Human, Earth Project' team for their ongoing efforts.

Last but not least, a huge thank you to everyone who played a role in this story and made it possible. Some of you are named in the text, and some of you are not – you know who you are.

**Part one of the incredible true story behind
the acclaimed 'Sisters for Sale' documentary**

EVERY STRANGER'S EYES

BY BEN RANDALL

Following the mysterious abductions of his local
friends May and Pang, an Australian filmmaker
returns to Vietnam determined to do everything
he can to find and help them.

'Every Stranger's Eyes' is a powerful and deeply
personal account illustrating the importance of
direct action and the dangers of losing sight
of what you believe in.

Learn more at www.sistersforsale.com

ISBN: 978-0-6487573-1-3 (paperback),
978-0-6487573-0-6 (PDF), 978-0-6487573-2-0 (epub)

**Part three of the incredible true story behind
the acclaimed 'Sisters for Sale' documentary**

THE MAN'S MACHINE

BY BEN RANDALL

An Australian filmmaker struggles to find his
kidnapped friends May and Pang in the immensity
of China, where they have been forced into
marriage with local men.

With his two-man team rapidly falling apart
and a near-impossible time limit, he discovers a
strange web of hidden connections leading
back to May's family in Vietnam.

Learn more at www.sistersforsale.com

SISTERS FOR SALE

THE HUMAN, EARTH PROJECT

ISBN: 978-0-6487573-7-5 (paperback),
978-0-6487573-6-8 (PDF), 978-0-6487573-8-2 (epub)